STYLE/HACKING

Sew a Creative Wardrobe

Use 5 Favorite Garments for Limitless Possibilities

Karoline Dahrling Hughes

stashBOOKS®

an imprint of C&T Publishing

Text, photography, and artwork copyright © 2021 by Karoline Dahrling Hughes

PUBLISHER: Amy Barrett-Daffin

CREATIVE DIRECTOR: Gailen Runge

ACQUISITIONS EDITOR: Roxane Cerda

MANAGING EDITOR: Liz Aneloski

EDITOR: Beth Baumgartel

TECHNICAL EDITOR: Helen Frost

COVER/BOOK DESIGNER: April Mostek

PRODUCTION COORDINATOR: Zinnia Heinzmann

PRODUCTION EDITOR: Jennifer Warren

ILLUSTRATOR: Karoline Dahrling Hughes

PHOTO ASSISTANTS: Lauren Herberg and Gabriel Martinez

PHOTOGRAPHY by Karoline Dahrling Hughes, unless otherwise noted

Published by Stash Books, an imprint of C&T Publishing, Inc., P.O. Box 1456, Lafayette, CA 94549

Attention Teachers: C&T Publishing, Inc., encourages the use of our books as texts for teaching. You can find lesson plans for many of our titles at ctpub.com or contact us at ctinfo@ctpub.com.

We take great care to ensure that the information included in our products is accurate and presented in good faith, but no warranty is provided, nor are results guaranteed. Having no control over the choices of materials or procedures used, neither the author nor C&T Publishing, Inc., shall have any liability to any person or entity with respect to any loss or damage caused directly or indirectly by the information contained in this book. For your convenience, we post an up-to-date listing of corrections on our website (ctpub.com). If a correction is not already noted, please contact our customer service department at ctinfo@ctpub.com or P.O. Box 1456, Lafayette, CA 94549.

Trademark (™) and registered trademark (®) names are used throughout this book. Rather than use the symbols with every occurrence of a trademark or registered trademark name, we are using the names only in the editorial fashion and to the benefit of the owner, with no intention of infringement.

Library of Congress Cataloging-in-Publication Data

Names: Hughes, Karoline Dahrling, author.

Title: Stylehacking, sew a creative wardrobe : use 5 favorite garments for limitless possibilities / Karoline Dahrling Hughes.

Description: Lafayette, CA : Stash Books, an imprint of C&T Publishing, 2021.

Identifiers: LCCN 2021032163 | ISBN 9781644031148 (trade paperback) | ISBN 9781644031155 (ebook)

Subjects: LCSH: Dressmaking--Pattern design. | Sewing.

Classification: LCC TT520 .H893 2021 | DDC 646.4--dc23

LC record available at https://lccn.loc.gov/2021032163

Printed in the USA

10 9 8 7 6 5 4 3 2 1

Dedication

TO JOLINA AND ROXIE. YOU WILL ALWAYS BE THE BEST DAUGHTERS
I COULD EVER WISH FOR.

AND TO MY BROTHER KASPER. I WILL MISS YOU FOREVER.
I KNOW THIS BOOK WOULD HAVE MADE YOU PROUD.

Acknowledgments

It takes more than one simple sewing girl to write a book like this.

To my mother, Lina, and to Peter, Mick, and Louise: Thank you for always supporting me and helping make anything possible. A special thanks goes to Lina for all the ironing and all the love.

Thanks to Jolina and Roxie for believing in me and sharing their excitement. Additional thanks to Jolina for helping me take some of the photos. She is one of the youngest sewing-book photographers—of that I am sure!

A sincere thank-you to my great friends for cheering me on and for listening when I was close to giving up.

Thanks also to the KreaKlub for all the nights of inspiration and hygge.

Thank you, Roxane, Liz, and the rest of C&T Publishing, for believing in this idea.

My appreciation to the English family for showing me there is such a kind world outside little Hjørring.

Thanks to my dear old grandparents Sonja and Palle for giving me a sewing machine, time, inspiration, and love.

Many thanks to my wonderful models—Jolina, Roxie, Lina, Lotte, Alan, Anne-Sofie, Mai, Lillian, Maja, Villum, Mia, Kathrine, Amalie, and Mary Anne—you all helped me bring this book to life by being so amazing and perfect just the way you are.

Thanks to the kind people at the fantastic art museum in Hjørring, Vendsyssel Kunstmusem (vkm.dk), for allowing us to take photographs at such a beautiful location.

Last but not least, thank you, Alan, for helping me remember that working hard to achieve your dream is just a good thing. And for sorting out my back when it was aching from cutting, sewing, and writing.

CONTENTS

INTRODUCTION: MY JOURNEY

I HAVE ALWAYS BEEN CREATIVE AND I HAVE ALWAYS LOVED TO SEW. ALWAYS.

I was not great at it at first, but I just kept trying. I made things: dresses out of duvet covers, skirts from tablecloths, jackets from curtains. And sometimes I even made things with material from my mum's small and precious fabric stash. She was kind to let me do that because she did not have very much.

When I was thirteen years old, my beloved grandmother, Sonja, gave me her old sewing machine. It was my very own machine, and I remember travelling home with it on the plane from her house on the little island where I had visited her.

I got home at midnight and went straight to my room to sew all through the night. The next day I wore a very strange pair of trousers to school, ones that I had measured from a pair of trousers already in my closet.

And since then I have had a love affair with designing and making clothes.

I went to design school and learned all the tricks in pattern making, the details, the delicate skills, and all the endless paper pattern pieces that I often needed to make a single thing. I wanted to learn about pattern making and clothing design to see if it was for me. But I always went back to my own patternless method of making clothes, my quick-and-fast method of measuring from clothes I already had to whip up something nice and uniquely mine.

I love my design methods because I am not a perfectionist, because I want it to be fun, and because I am driven by quick results. I sometimes wish I had the interest and patience to devote the hours, days, months to complete a perfectly tailored dress with darts, invisible seams, hand-stitched edges, and so on. I see the results other people have and they are beautiful. But that is not me. I would like to make something now, and put it on in a mere hour or two.

Welcome to This Book

This book is for those of you who have never dared to sew before and for those of you who have been stopped in your attempts by the many sheets of papers in a pattern envelope, with oh so much to understand about the lines, the darts, and even the seam allowances.

I hope you are looking at this book because you cannot wait to get started being creative. Perhaps you already show your creativity with yourself and your outfits. Perhaps you have been making things for years and years, or perhaps you just have a dream about learning how to sew your own clothes. This book is for you.

I wrote this book because I want you to feel the joy of fuss-free creativity.

The idea of styleHacking and the projects in this book are made for quick results. I hope they will help you feel the joy of sewing. There are no ball gowns with endless details, no waisted jackets or trousers with perfect fit. There are *wonderful*, quick styles to make in a jiffy. Remember it can be simple and still be beautiful!

You cannot make everything with the styleHacking method, but you sure can do a lot. Enjoy the freedom of it, create details in your unique way, and embrace the styles that work well for you.

Embrace the fact that this method sewing is for everyone! All it takes is to jump in and dare to cut into that fabric. The joy of magically making a piece of clothing on your sewing machine will almost certainly last longer than the joy that comes with the instant gratification of a shopping fix. Even though it is sewn quickly, it is still a good way to relieve stress. In just a couple of hours you can unwind and create something to wear later that day. I promise you: You will reach sewing zen with your sewing machine!

Get ready to experience the joy of creating, the pride of wearing things you stitched together, and the wonder of having the wardrobe of your dreams.

GETTING STARTED

It doesn't take a lot to get started, but it does help to be prepared. Here are a few things to keep in mind.

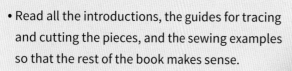

- Make a comfortable space for sewing. Put on nice music or set up your space close to friends and family so you can chat and be cozy. If you can leave works in progress set up, all the better.

- Don't worry if you do not have a fancy sewing machine. A straight stitch and a zigzag stitch are really all you need.

- Read all the introductions, the guides for tracing and cutting the pieces, and the sewing examples so that the rest of the book makes sense.

- You might mess up. Do not give up, even if you forget the extra width for seam allowances, turn your printed fabric the wrong way, or cut the wrong way! Mistakes happen.

  Turn them into something else and try again. And then, suddenly, you are styleHacking without even thinking about the rules on how to do it! Never give up.

- Wear your handmade pieces! Remember to be proud of the clothes you have made and use them to express your personal style.

What You Need

Many sewing books feature several pages listing the things you need and how those things work. I always skip those pages to get to the more interesting pages, but the tools that make sewing easier are important, so here is a list of tools and supplies to have on hand.

TOOLS AND SUPPLIES

Sewing machine: There is no need to be picky. If your machine can do straight and zigzag stitching, it will work fine. Once you start sewing your own clothes, perhaps you will have spent less money on clothes, and then there will be money for a machine upgrade.

Tip

I have a serger because I am such a lazy girl and I like to finish my projects quickly. I use the serger to finish all the edges and internal stitches so the inside of the garment looks as nice as the outside. But that is pure luxury, and you can easily get by without one; just use a zigzag stitch.

Fabric scissors (good sharp ones)

Thread: Sometimes I don't even bother to find matching thread. If anybody asks if it does not match on purpose, I just answer yes.

Seam ripper

Measuring tape

Hand and sewing machine needles

Safety pins: These are great for when you need to insert ribbons or elastic through casing.

Pins or Wonder Clips (by Clover)

Tailor's chalk or fabric markers: These ensure you make a mistake while drawing and not while cutting.

Paper scissors

Cardboard, poster board, or large pieces of stiff paper: You'll use these to make your styleHack basic templates. Tape several pieces together to make larger templates.

For some of the styles, you will need sewing notions such as **elastic, bias tape,** or **knitted tape.** The various styles make note of any special needs.

Just use your imagination and get started.

FABRIC

Start your styleHacking journey with inexpensive fabric. It will reduce a lot of stress. Use old tablecloths and duvet covers, find a good sale at a fabric store, or even search for vintage materials at the thrift shop. Often very fun clothes come from found fabric.

Sewing and making clothes yourself can also be a small step toward a more sustainable lifestyle. You can buy fabric produced under controlled and certified conditions, and you can find materials secondhand. Remember that a beautiful old tablecloth, lovely bed linen, or piece of thrift-store clothing can be made into amazing new stuff. And save those leftover bits and scraps! They are almost always useful.

Types of Fabric

The projects in this book are suitable for a variety of fabrics: woven and stretch fabrics, thin and thick fabrics, and for all kinds of textures. Some styles can be made from both woven and stretch fabrics, while others are better made from one or the other. If the style is roomy, then the fabric doesn't need to stretch; but if the style is fitted, it will need to be made with stretch fabrics. The project descriptions indicate the most suitable fabrics. It is a good idea to become familiar with different fabrics, touch them, drape them over your arm, and get accustomed to how they hang and behave. Try identifying the fabrics of some of your favorite clothes and see if they are the fabrics that you prefer.

Knit fabrics are easy to wear since they stretch when you put them on, but you do have to be a bit more careful when sewing with them because they tend to shift and stretch. Some knits only stretch in one direction and some stretch in both directions.

Tip

Make sure to position the pattern templates on the fabric so the fabric stretches the most across the garment (and not vertically).

Woven fabrics can be found in so many fibers, weaves, qualities, and costs. Enjoy the search and exploration of fabric, and don't forget to shop thrifty.

Tip

It is always a good idea to wash and iron your fabric before cutting and sewing the garment. That way you make sure the fabric shrinks instead of your dress shrinking. It's especially important to wash new fabric because sometimes it shrinks more than you would expect. It's always good to be on the safe side!

Making the Most of Your Fabric

This book does not provide the exact amount of fabric needed for a specific style for a certain size, but you will quickly learn how to see what you can make from a piece of fabric.

The best way to make sure you have enough fabric or to know how much you need to buy is to lay out the template for the garment you want to make on a table and measure the length and the width at the widest point.

When you purchase fabric, it usually comes in 45″ (114cm) or 60″ (152cm) widths. When you find fabulous fabric of an undetermined width, you'll need to determine exactly how wide and long it is before you start cutting it. You want to make sure you'll have enough fabric to make the intended garment.

For example: 60″ (152cm)-wide fabric can be folded with a single fold or with 2 folds. A single fold creates 2 layers of fabric, while 2 folds make 4 layers of fabric.

- For sizes up to and including US 12, several of the styles will fit on a single 60″ (152cm) width of fabric. If you are making a larger size, you might need twice as much fabric.

For example: 45″ (114cm)-wide fabric can usually only be folded once.

- Unless you are making something very small, like a top, and you only need to cut a front piece or a back piece on one width of fabric, you will probably need more yardage—sometimes twice as much as wider fabric. You will quickly learn approximately how much fabric you need to make the various projects for your size.

- If the patterns fit on one width of fabric, you will need the length measurement of the project plus the seam allowance. If, for example, you are making a sleeveless dress and can fit both the front and back piece on one width of wide fabric, and you want the dress to be 30″ (76cm) long, you only need a 30″ (76cm) length of fabric, plus seam allowances.

- If the fabric is narrow and can only fit either the front or back on one width of fabric, you need twice the length measurement of the project. If you want to make a sleeveless dress that is 30″ (76cm) long, you'll need a 60″ (152cm) length of fabric, plus seam allowances. With a bit more fabric, you might have an opportunity to add sleeves to the dress or make the skirt wider!

- Some of the styles need to be cut from 60″ (152cm)-wide fabric whatever the size. These include the tube skirt, the circle skirt, and the poncho.

There are several ways to fold the fabric in preparation for cutting out the patterns.

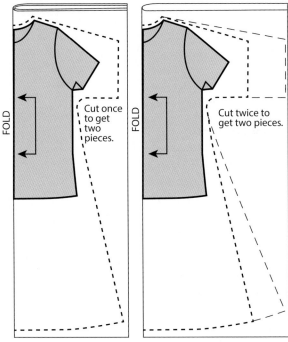

The width of the fabric will yield a basic dress shape or a wider dress shape with longer sleeves.

For 60″ (152cm)-wide fabric:

- **1 fold, 2 layers:** Fold vertically with 1 center fold so there are 2 layers, each 30″ (75cm) wide.

- **2 folds, 4 layers:** Fold vertically in the middle, just like the first folding method, and then vertically in the middle again, for a width of 15″ (38cm). This works for very narrow styles, and you can cut once and get both the front and back pieces.

For 45″ (114cm)-wide fabric:

- **1 fold, 2 layers:** Fold vertically in the middle so there are 2 layers, each 22½″ (57cm).

Sometimes, you need to be creative when cutting the templates. I often think of it as a challenge to make the most of the fabric I have.

Some tips:

- Fold wide fabrics twice to make tops or dresses with short sleeves. Fold narrow fabrics once and you'll have a bit more fabric to make the sleeves longer.

- The templates for some of the narrower trousers and leggings in this book will fit on one width of fabric folded once; however, wider trouser styles probably will need 2 lengths of fabric.

- Some of the styles feature wide sleeves or a lot of ruffles, and the amount of fabric needed for these styles depends completely on the size, the style, and the fabric width. It is a bit trickier to determine the correct yardage, but over time you will start to know. I advise you to buy cheaper fabrics or large materials from thrift shops to get a sense on how to place the templates and get as much as possible from your fabric.

SEWING TECHNIQUES

There are several techniques you will use repeatedly to make all the styleHack projects. They are easy to master through practice.

Basic Stitches

All the projects are sewn with either a straight or zigzag stitch. If your machine has a stretch stitch, that is helpful, but a zigzag stitch will work too.

Straight stitch: Use a normal straight stitch for sewing pieces of fabric together and for hemming.

Zigzag stitch: Use this stitch to sew seams or hems that need to stretch and to finish fabric edges to minimize fraying.

Serger: If you have a serger, you can use it to finish seam allowances and exposed edges. You can also use some sergers to seam, which makes the sewing process very quick since the serger seams, trims, and finishes the seam allowances all at the same time.

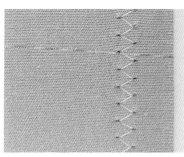

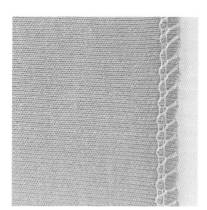

Tip

If you don't want to zigzag or serge the edges of the fabric, you can use pinking shears to help stop the cut edge from fraying.

Hemming

SINGLE-FOLD HEM

Since the hem edge is exposed, you might want to serge or zigzag the raw edges.

1 Fold the fabric ½″ (1.3cm) to the wrong side. Press the fold; pin it in place or use Wonder Clips.

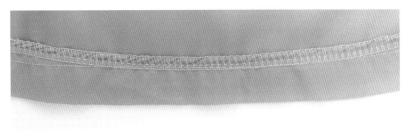

2 Stitch the fold in place using a normal stitch seam and getting as close to the edge of the fabric as possible. Or hem with 2 rows of parallel stitching. You can use a twin needle if your machine can hold one, or you can stitch the 2 rows approximately ⅙″ (4mm) apart.

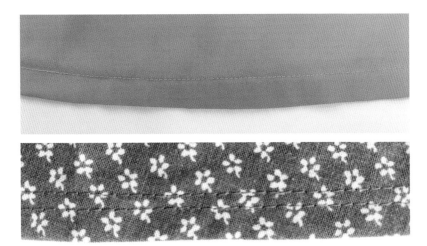

Tip

Use a zigzag stitch or stretch stitch to hem knit or stretch fabrics. You can also use decorative stretch stitches if your sewing machine has the capability.

DOUBLE-FOLD HEM

For this type of hem, it is not necessary to zigzag or serge the raw edges of the fabric, since they will be hidden inside the hem.

1 Fold the fabric ¼″ (6mm) to the wrong side and press.

2 Fold the fabric again ¼″ (6mm) to the wrong side and press.

3 Stitch the fold in place as close to the edge of the fold as possible.

ZIGZAG EDGE

Sew with a zigzag stitch very close to the edge. This gives a different effect and works really well on some types of fabric. It is a good finish for ruffles where folded fabric might make the hem look stiff.

Edge Finishes

There are several ways to finish a garment edge other than hemming. These include decorative edgings as well as finishing techniques for waistbands and other openings.

BIAS TAPE

1 Open the bias tape and fold one narrow end of the bias tape so the wrong sides are together. Pin or clip the bias tape to the fabric with right sides together and edges aligned. Stitch along the fold in the bias tape closest to the edge.

2 Extend the bias tape away from the seam and toward the wrong side of the fabric. Fold it closed to hide the seam. Pin or clip the bias tape in place.

3 Stitch the bias tape close to the other fold of the bias tape.

Wrong side of finished edge

Right side of finished edge

INSIDE OUT

Folding the fabric to the right side creates a unique finish that almost looks like bias tape but stretches with your fabric.

1 Fold the fabric ¼″ (6mm) or narrower to the right side and press.

2 Fold the fabric again ¼″ (6mm) to the right side and press.

3 Stitch in place as close to the edge of the fold as possible.

Tip

Since the seams will show, use thread in a fun color to add a little extra touch.

KNITTED TAPE

Applying knitted tape is much like applying bias tape, except the knitted tape doesn't have pressed folds.

1 Pin or clip the tape to the garment edge with right sides together. Stitch ¼″–½″ (6cm–13cm) from the raw edge.

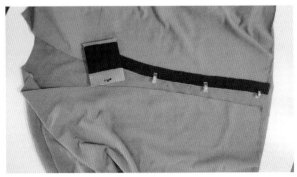

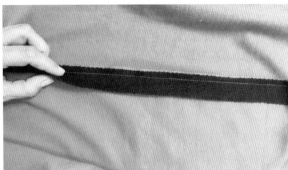

2 Fold the tape toward the wrong side. The choice is yours on how much of the tape you want to be visible. You can fold it completely to the wrong side or leave part of it showing so it looks like a piped edge.

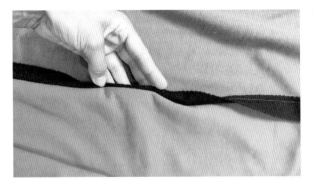

3 Pin or clip the tape in place and stitch.

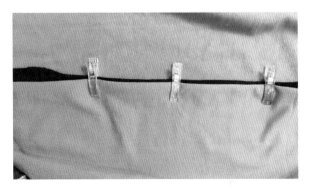

Wrong side of finished edge

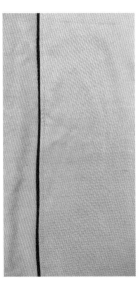
Right side of finished edge

Tip

You can also use a rectangular piece of knit fabric in place of knitted tape (page 24). Fold the fabric rectangle in half and apply it like knitted tape.

DECORATIVE CUFFS

Ribbed knit fabric, designed for binding edges that need to stretch, is available in many decorative options. Use a stretch or zigzag stitch or a serger.

1 Cut the cuffs so they are a bit smaller than the sleeve opening. Stitch the cuffs with right sides together to make a small tube.

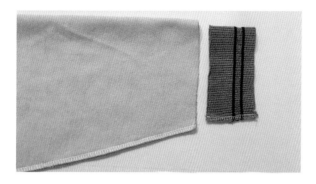

2 Pin or clip the cuff to the opening with right sides together so that the edges are aligned, as shown.

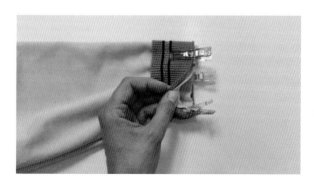

3 Stitch the cuff to the sleeve opening, stretching it evenly all around.

FABRIC BANDS

Fabric bands are an easy finish for necklines, sleeves, or bottom openings. They should be made from knit fabric for garments made of knits that need to stretch. You can use woven fabrics for garments that are cut looser, like the kimono (page 116), and don't need to stretch. Use a stretch or zigzag stitch or a serger to attach knit bands.

1 Cut a long rectangular piece of fabric for the band. Measure where the band will be (neckline, waist, wrist, or ankle) as well as the garment opening to determine the band measurement.

Width: 2 times the desired height plus 2 times the seam allowance

Length for a neckline, wrist, or ankle: Stretch the opening, measure, and then cut the fabric slightly shorter than the opening. The band should be stretched a bit when stitched.

Length for a sleeve opening or bottom hem: Cut the band the same length as the opening or slightly shorter.

 Tip

Never make a fabric band larger than the opening to which it will be stitched.

2 With right sides together, stitch the narrow ends of the fabric band to form a tube.

3 Fold the band in half with wrong sides together, so the right side of the fabric faces out.

4 Pin or clip the band to the right side of the opening as shown.

5 Stitch the band to the opening, stretching it evenly all around.

Wrong side of finished edge

Right side of finished edge

FABRIC BANDS WITH ELASTIC

Another edge-finish option when you need it to stretch is to create a fabric band to hold a length of elastic. Use a stretch or zigzag stitch or a serger.

1 Cut a long rectangular piece of fabric.

   Width: 2 times the desired height plus 2 times seam allowance

   Length: Measure and then cut the fabric slightly shorter than the opening it will be stitched onto.

2 Measure where the band will be (waist, wrist, or ankle) as well as the garment opening to determine the band measurement. For a tube top, measure the bodice. Cut a piece of elastic to the measurement.

3 Check that the elastic and fabric band fit around the garment opening. With right sides together, stitch the narrow ends of the rectangle together to form a circle. Overlap and stitch the ends of the elastic to form a circle.

4 Fold the band in half with wrong sides together to form a tube. Place the elastic inside the folded tube. Make sure the elastic isn't twisted.

5 Pin or clip the band to the opening with right sides together and the edges aligned. Stitch the band to the opening, stretching it evenly all around.

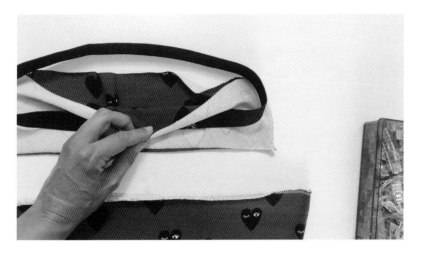

 Tip

To make it a bit easier to stitch the band to the garment opening, stitch the raw edges of the band together first, with the elastic inside.

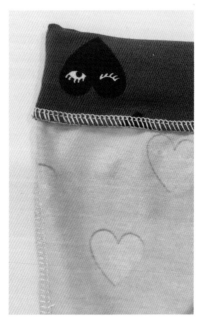

Wrong side of finished edge

Right side of finished edge

DECORATIVE ELASTIC

A piece of decorative elastic is a great looking and easy way to finish a style. Use a stretch or zigzag stitch or a serger.

1 Measure where the elastic will be (waist, wrist, or ankle) as well as the garment opening to determine the elastic measurement. Cut the elastic so it is slightly smaller than the measurement and slightly smaller than the piece to which it will be attached.

2 Overlap and stitch the ends of the elastic to form a circle.

3 Zigzag or serge the raw edge of the fabric where the elastic will be attached to make sure the edge doesn't fray. If the garment has a center back seam, align the seam of the elastic with the seam of the garment. If the garment doesn't have a center back seam, measure and mark the center back of the garment, and then align the elastic seam with the center marking. Pin or clip the elastic to the garment opening with right sides together.

4 Stitch the elastic to the opening using a zigzag stitch, stretching it evenly all around.

Wrong side of finished edge

Right side of finished edge

ELASTIC CASING

Creating a casing in the garment edge to hold a length of elastic is an easy way to finish the style. It does require adding extra fabric to the length (or height) of the garment edge before cutting out the pieces.

1 Measure the width of the elastic, and calculate 2 times the elastic width plus the seam allowance to know how much to add to the top of the waist. If, for instance, the elastic is 1″ (2.5cm) wide and the seam allowance is ½″, add 2½″ (6.3cm) to the top of the waist so there is enough fabric to create a fabric casing for the elastic.

2 Construct the garment until it is time to finish the garment edge. Finish the raw edge of the opening with a zigzag or overlock stitch.

3 Measure around yourself at the location of the elastic casing. Cut the elastic to that measurement plus ½″ (1.3cm).

4 Fold and press the opening edge (the amount determined in Step 1) to the wrong side.

5 Pin or clip the fold in place. Zigzag stitch along the raw edge to create the casing. Leave a small gap in the stitching for inserting the elastic.

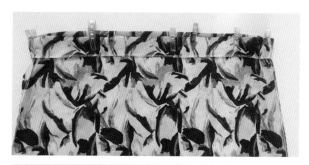

6 Attach a safety pin to one end of the elastic, and work the elastic into the opening, through the casing, and out the opening. You might want to clip or pin the loose end of the elastic to the outside of the casing so it doesn't pull through.

7 Once the elastic has gone all the way through, make sure it isn't twisted inside the casing. Overlap and stitch the ends of the elastic to form a circle.

8 Stitch the opening closed.

Right side of finished edge

Gathering Fabric

Gathers are tiny soft folds that add shape and fullness to a garment.

CUTTING THE FABRIC TO GATHER

The gathered fabric piece should be cut significantly wider than the fabric piece to which it will be attached, like a skirt to a waistband or like a full ruffle to the bottom of a skirt. Depending on how full you want the garment piece or the ruffle, the extra width can be 1½–2 times wider than the garment edge, depending sometimes on much fabric you have. Heavier-weight fabrics work best with less extra width, while lightweight fabrics gather up more easily and can be fuller.

FORMING GATHERS

1 Cut the fabric piece that will be gathered to the desired width.

2 Stitch 2 parallel rows of basting stitches on the top edge.

3 Pull the bobbin threads to gather up the fabric to make small folds.

4 Adjust the gathers so they are evenly distributed to fit the smaller garment piece.

5 Pin or clip the pieces with right sides together, and stitch them with a regular-length straight stitch.

MAKING RUFFLES

Try this styleHack to add ruffles to the bottom of sleeves quickly and easily without any basting stitches.

In this example, the sleeve ruffles are 4˝ long and about 1½ times wider than the sleeve opening.

1 Cut the fabric piece for the ruffle.

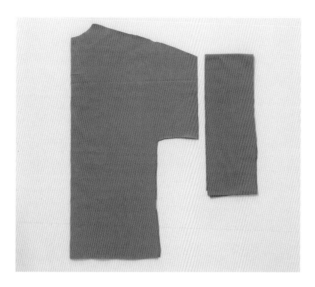

3 Pin or clip the ruffle fabric evenly around the garment opening with right sides together. Use lots of pins and clips.

2 With right sides together, stitch the narrow ends together to form a tube.

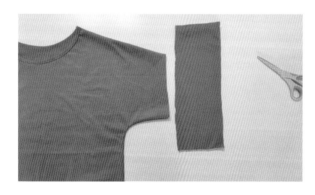

4 Using a straight stitch, sew the ruffled piece to the sleeve opening. Finish the seam with a zigzag stitch or use a serger.

Tip: Hand Baste to Form Gathers

Optionally, to help make sure the gathers are easier to control and are evenly distributed, you can hand baste the top edge of the ruffle fabric. Use a hand needle and thread to form long straight stitches along the fabric edge. Then gently pull the thread to tighten the stitches and gather up the fabric to the desired width to match the sleeve opening. Make sure the folds are evenly spaced when you attach the gathered piece.

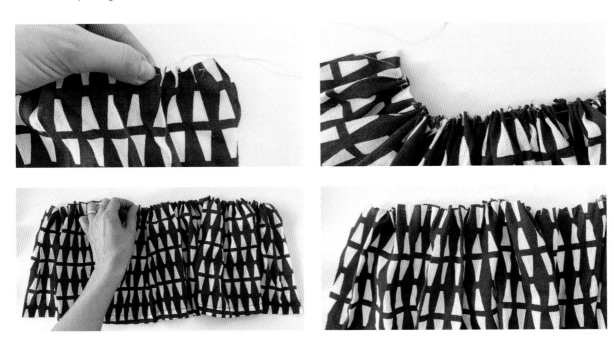

Making a Tiered Skirt

You can add ruffles to any garment edge! A good example is a 3-tiered skirt, with each tier cut and attached to the adjacent tier just like ruffles.

• Cut the first tier about 50″ (127cm) wide, which is a bit wider than the width of the waistband.

• Cut the second tier about double the width of the first tier: 100″ (254cm).

• Cut the third tier about double the width of the second tier: 200″ (508cm).

This is a lot of fabric—it can look beautiful, but it is also a lot of ruffles to manage when you are sewing. Keep this in mind when you decide how many tiers or layers of ruffles you want to add to your design.

TRACING AND CUTTING THE 5 BASIC TEMPLATES

THERE ARE FIVE BASIC STYLE TEMPLATES—A TANK TOP, A T-SHIRT, A SWEATER, LEGGINGS, AND TROUSERS—THAT YOU CAN USE OR ADAPT TO MAKE EVERY DESIGN SHOWN IN THIS BOOK.

This chapter shows you how to make the basic templates and then shows you how to adapt each template for a style variation. You'll find that some of the 35+ styles in the project section can be made by simply using the marking and cutting techniques shown here. Other styles have additional steps, covered in the project instructions.

Please read the tracing and cutting instructions carefully so you have the best possible understanding of the technique. They make styleHacking quick, easy, and so much fun.

Making a Full Template

Most of the garment styles in this book are made from a half-template, meant for placing on the fold of the fabric, but for some you'll want to start with a full template. Here are 2 ways to make a full template.

- Start with the half-template. Trace 2 copies, add the markings, and cut them out. Tape the 2 half-templates together along the center front or center back to make a full template.

- Start with the half-template. Fold a piece of paper in half, aligning the paper fold with the center back or center front, and trace the template on the paper. Open the paper for a full template and add the markings.

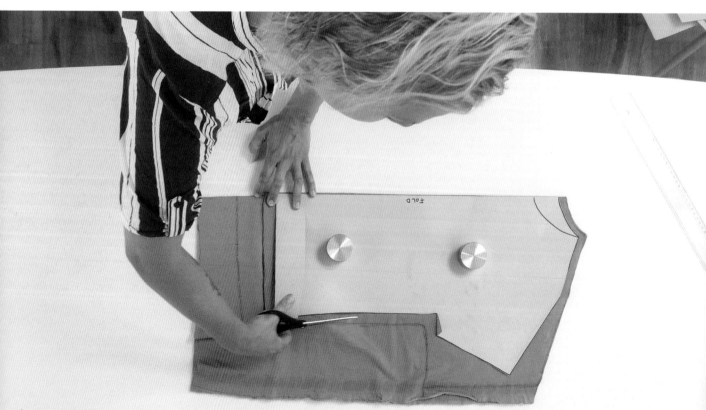

Make a Tank Top Template

Find a tank top that is not too tight and is made with moderately stretchy fabric. Avoid tank tops made in synthetic stretch fabrics that have so much elasticity that they are very small when folded.

Many commercially made tank tops have uneven side seams after washing, so iron the one you are going to use and gently stretch and shape it so it is as even and symmetrical as possible.

1 Fold the tank top in half vertically and place the center fold against a straight edge of the paper or cardboard. There is no seam allowance necessary along the fold line.

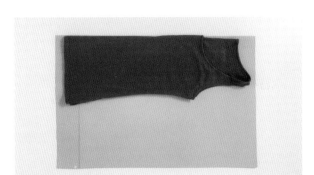

2 Mark all the way around the tank top with a pencil. If the straps are not right on top of each other, mark around them both. If the garment has a high back, carefully fold it down and mark where the front straps are.

3 Remove the tank top. Mark the lines with a bold marker. Even out the lines if your garment was not completely straight. Don't add the seam allowance yet; you'll add it when you place the template on your fabric.

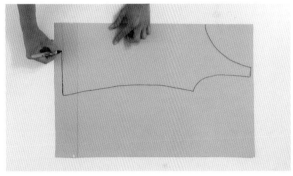

4 Cut on the markings to finish the tank top template. Mark the fold line.

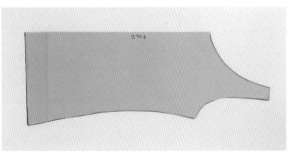

USING THE TANK TOP TEMPLATE TO CUT A TUBE TOP

Use stretch fabric. Fold the fabric in half lengthwise; then fold or layer again so you are cutting 4 layers.

1 Place the template on top of the fabric with the fold edge aligned with the fabric fold.

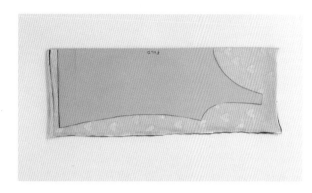

2 Fold down the top of the template at the bottom of the armhole and top of the side seam.

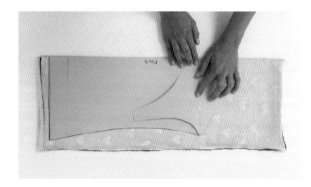

3 Mark ½″–¾″ (1.3–1.9cm) seam allowances on all the edges.

4 Mark a rectangle for the fabric band with elastic that will be sewn to the top of the garment. Mark a piece that is 2 times the desired width (the height) of the band plus 2 times the seam allowance. The length should be ½″–1″ (1.3–2.5cm) smaller than the width of the tube top itself.

In this example, the desired width is 1½″ (3.8cm) and the seam allowance is ½″ (1.3cm):

2 × 1½″ (3.8cm) + 2 × ½″ (1.3cm) = total cut width

3″ (7.6cm) + 1″ (2.5cm) = 4″ (10.1cm)

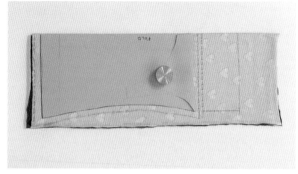

Tip

When you begin styleHacking, use a more generous seam allowance so there is more wiggle room in case the fabric of the new garment is not as stretchy as the traced garment. You can always sew the garment a bit tighter with a wider seam allowance, but you can't sew it looser!

5 Cut on the markings to make 1 tube top front, 1 tube top back, and 2 fabric bands.

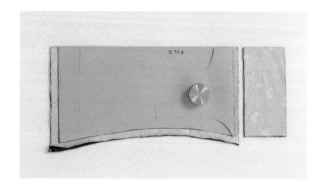

Make a T-Shirt Template

This template has an integrated sleeve that is a continuation of the front and back pieces instead of a separate piece.

Find a T-shirt that is not too tight and is made with moderately stretchy fabric. Many commercially made T-shirts have uneven side seams after washing, so iron the one you are going to use and gently stretch and shape it so it is as even and symmetrical as possible.

1 Fold the T-shirt in half vertically and place the center fold against a straight edge of the paper or cardboard. There is no seam allowance necessary along the fold line.

3 Remove the T-shirt. Mark the lines with a bold marker. Even out the lines if the garment was not completely straight. Don't add the seam allowance yet; you'll add it when you place the template on your fabric.

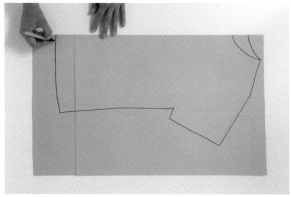

2 Mark the lines with a pencil. Mark around the back neck of the T-shirt first and then lift the neck a bit to mark the front neck of the T-shirt as well. Trace the sleeve.

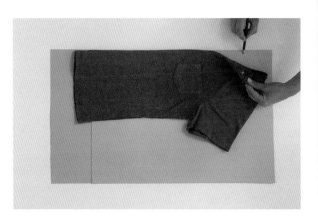

4 Cut on the markings to finish the T-shirt template. Mark the fold line.

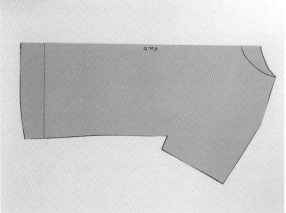

USING THE T-SHIRT TEMPLATE TO CUT A T-SHIRT

Use stretch fabric. Fold the fabric in half lengthwise; then fold or layer again so you are cutting 4 layers.

1 Place the T-shirt template on top of the fabric with the fold edge aligned with the fold of the fabric.

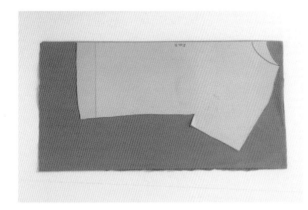

2 Fold up the bottom arm opening so you can mark a right angle around it.

3 Mark ½″–¾″ (1.3–1.9cm) seam allowances on the neck, side, and bottom edges. For the back template, adjust the markings from the shoulder seam and around the sleeve for a wider arm sleeve opening, as shown. With these adjustments, the marked sleeve opening should be larger than the sleeve opening of the actual T-shirt template.

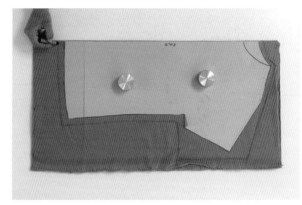

Tip

Narrow ½″–¾″ (1.3–1.9cm) seam allowances will make a tight-fitting T-shirt. You can mark a wider seam allowance along the sides of the template for a boxy fit. You can also make the T-shirt shorter or longer by making the cutting line longer or shorter than the template. It's up to you, and there are several examples of longer and shorter style variations in the book. In this example, the T-shirt is a bit shorter than the template.

It's also a good idea to add a more generous seam allowance so there is extra fabric in case the fabric of the new garment is not as stretchy as the traced garment. You can always sew the garment a bit tighter with a wider seam allowance, but you can't sew it looser!

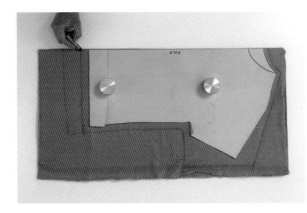

4 Cut on the markings.

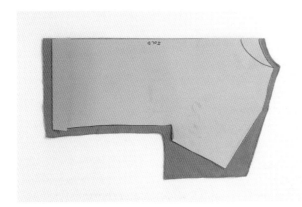

5 Take the template off and remove the top folded fabric layer. This is the T-shirt back piece.

6 Place the template back on the remaining folded piece of fabric. Mark the front neckline.

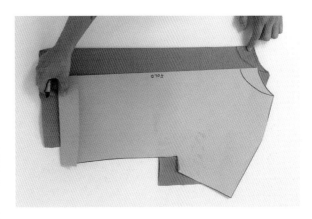

7 Add a ½"–¾" (1.3–1.9cm) seam allowance to the new neckline marking. Cut the excess fabric away. This is the T-shirt front piece.

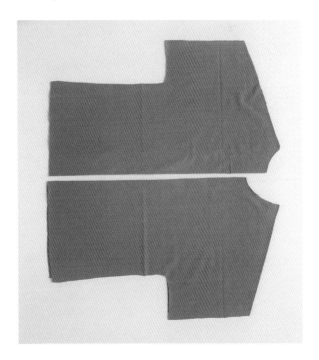

Make a Sweater Template

This template has a separate sleeve template.

Find a sweater that is not too tight and is made with moderately stretchy fabric. Many commercially made sweaters have uneven side seams after washing, so iron the one you are going to use and gently stretch and shape it so it is as even and symmetrical as possible.

1 Fold the sweater in half vertically and place the center fold right up against a straight side of the paper or cardboard. There is no seam allowance necessary along the fold line.

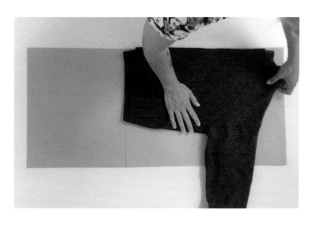

2 Fold in the sleeves of the sweater to follow the side seam, even if that is not where the sleeve seam is. Mark all the way around the sweater with a pencil.

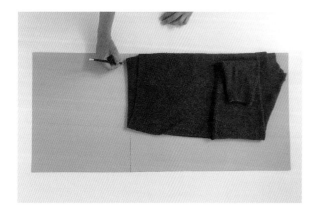

3 Mark around the back neck of the sweater and then lift the neck a bit to mark the front neck of the sweater as well.

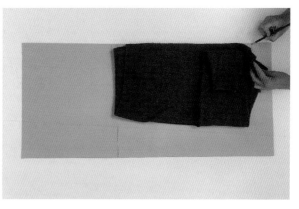

4 Remove the sweater. Mark the lines with a bold marker. Even out the lines if the garment was not completely straight. Don't add the seam allowance yet; you'll add it when you place the template on your fabric.

5 Place the sleeve on a new piece of paper or cardboard. Align the paper edge with the sweater side seam and begin the sleeve template there, even though that does not follow the sleeve seam of the sweater. Mark around the sleeve.

6 Mark the sleeve lines with a bold marker. Even out the lines if your garment was not completely straight. Don't add the seam allowance yet; you'll add it when you place the template on your fabric.

7 Cut on the markings to finish the sweater and sleeve templates. Mark the fold lines.

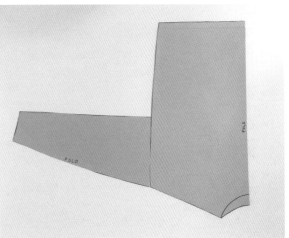

USING THE SWEATER TEMPLATE TO CUT A SWEATER

Use stretch fabric. Fold the fabric in half lengthwise; then fold or layer again so you are cutting 4 layers.

1 Place the templates on top of the fabric with the fold edge aligned with the fold of the fabric. If you want a shorter sweater or shorter sleeves, simply fold the template's bottom edge up. In this example, the template sleeve is folded up because a decorative cuff will be added.

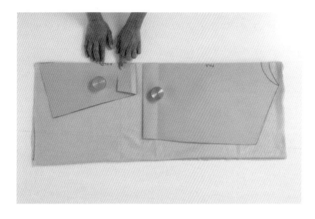

2 Mark ½″–¾″ (1.3–1.9cm) seam allowances on all the edges. Cut on the markings. Remove both sleeves and the top folded layer. This is the sweater back piece.

3 Place the back/front template back on the remaining folded piece of fabric. Lift the template, mark the front neckline on the fabric, and add a ½″–¾″ (1.3–1.9cm) seam allowance to the neckline. Cut the excess fabric away. This is the sweater front piece.

4 Cut on the markings to make 2 front pieces, 2 back pieces, and 2 sleeves.

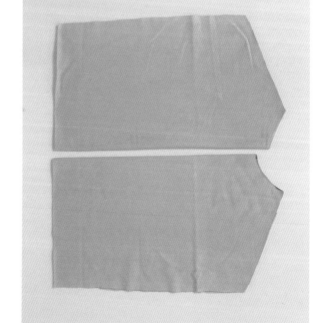

Tip

Do you have a wonderful fabric remnant, but the templates don't fit? Simply shorten the templates or take in the side seams slightly to make the templates fit. These simple changes make for a totally different sweater. This is styleHacking at its best!

Make a Leggings Template

First, find leggings are not too tight and are made with moderately stretchy fabric. Do not choose leggings made with 4-way stretch fabric or those made with Lycra that stretch a lot when you put them on. Many commercially made leggings have uneven side seams after washing, so iron the ones you are going to use and gently stretch and shape them so they are as even and symmetrical as possible.

1 To make the back template, fold the leggings in half vertically so the front of the leggings is facing out and place them on the paper or cardboard.

2 There most likely will be a big difference in the shape of the center front and back seams. It is important to trace the inner leg seam correctly, so for this you need to see where the inner leg seam is on the leggings. Measure how far the inner leg seam is from the edge of the fold. If the inner leg seam is, for example, 1″ (2.5cm) from the edge, then add an extra 1″ (2.5cm) from that fold. Then mark a curve and draw the back leggings template. Trace the back part of the leggings to mark the waist.

3 Mark around the leggings and the new inseam lines. Remove the leggings and mark the lines with a bold marker. Even out the lines if they are not completely straight. Don't add the seam allowance yet; you'll add it when you place the template on your fabric.

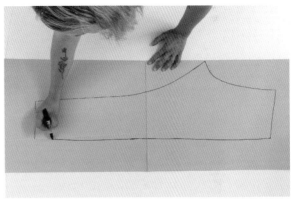

4 Cut on the markings to finish making the back template. Label the back template.

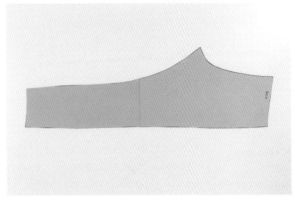

5 To make the front template, fold the leggings so the front of the leggings is facing out and place them on the paper or cardboard. It is important that you fold and place them correctly.

Fold the fabric in toward the back so it aligns with the inner leg seam. In Step 2, you added width to the inner seamline to make the back template, but for the front template, trace the inner seam exactly.

 Tip

It is easier to trace the inner leg seam if you fold the extra fabric back so it lies flat.

6 Trace the front waist by folding the back waist under so you have a clear edge to trace. This is because the center front seam is shorter than the center back seam.

Mark a curve and draw the front template.

7 Mark the lines with a bold marker. Even out the lines if your garment was not completely straight. Don't add the seam allowance yet; you'll add it when you place the template on your fabric.

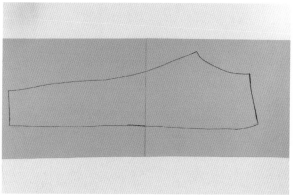

8 Cut on the markings to finish the front template. Label the front template.

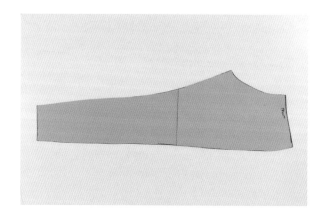

USING THE LEGGINGS TEMPLATE TO CUT LEGGINGS

Use stretch fabric. Fold the fabric in half lengthwise to make 2 layers. Some stretch fabrics only stretch in one direction, so make sure you place the leggings templates so the width of the templates follows the stretch of the fabric.

1 This layout, with the front template and back template placed top to bottom, saves fabric. However, if your fabric has a directional design, place the templates in the same direction.

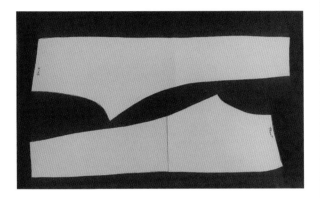

2 For a design variation with a decorative elastic waistband, consider these changes:

Higher waistline than the original leggings: Trace the templates as they are since the decorative elastic waistband will add height at the waist. Add extra if you want them higher.

Same waistline as original leggings: Fold down the templates at the waist. If the decorative elastic waistband is 2″ (5cm), then the amount to fold down at the waist is 2″ (5cm) minus ½″ (1.3cm) for the seam allowance. The total amount to fold down is 1½″ (3.8cm).

3 Mark ½″–¾″ (1.3–1.9cm) seam allowances on the edges. Mark the waistline as determined in Step 2.

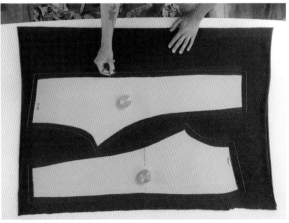

4 Cut on the markings to make 2 leggings front pieces and 2 leggings back pieces.

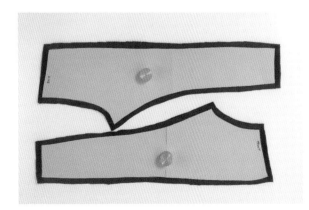

Make a Trousers Template

Find a pair of trousers that are loose fitting, or the trousers you make from templates will be too tight. This template works best to make loose-fitting jeans or pajama-style pants. Many commercially made trousers have uneven side seams after washing, so iron the ones you are going to use and gently stretch and shape them so they are as even and symmetrical as possible.

Follow Make a Leggings Template (page 41).

USING THE TROUSERS TEMPLATE TO CUT TROUSERS

Use stretch or woven fabric, folded in half lengthwise once, to make 2 layers.

1 For this style of trousers, you can plan to add a decorative elastic waistband. Decide if you want to change the placement of the waistline and make any adjustments following Using the Leggings Template to Cut Leggings, Step 2 (page 43). In this example, the template is folded down at the waist to keep the same waistline as the original trousers.

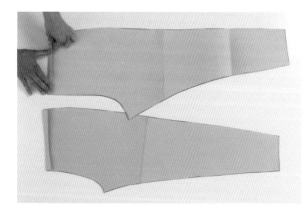

2 Place the trousers templates on top of the fabric. Since the fabric has a directional design, the templates face the same direction.

If you want the trouser legs to be wider, use a ruler to mark straight down from the knees to the hem directly on the fabric.

Mark ½″–¾″ (1.3–1.9cm) seam allowances on all the edges.

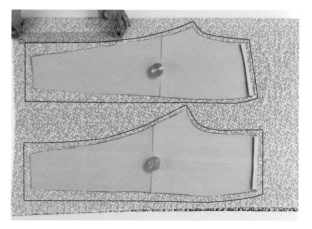

3 Cut on the markings to make 2 front pieces and 2 back pieces.

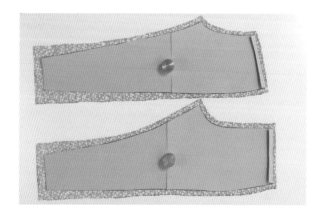

USING THE TROUSERS TEMPLATE TO CUT SKIRTS

Use the trousers back template to make a skirt. Fold the fabric in half lengthwise, then fold or layer again to make 4 layers.

1 Place the trousers back template on top of the fabric with the side seam aligned with the fold of the fabric. Fold the leg of the template up so it is 1″ (2.5cm) longer than you want the skirt to be.

2 For this style of skirt, you'll need to add a bit of height to the waistline so you can finish the top edge with an elastic casing. You will also need to draw skirt-shaped cutting lines.

• Measure the width of the elastic, and calculate 2 times the elastic width plus the seam allowance to know how much to add to the top of the waist. If the elastic is 1″ (2.5cm) wide, add 2½″ (6.3cm) to the top of the waist (see Elastic Casing, page 28).

• The skirt should start as a rectangular shape. The only rule is that the width of the widest part of the back template piece must be maintained so the skirt fits over the hips. Draw the design line slightly narrower, about 1″ (2.5cm), toward the top waist, and angle it outward from the widest point toward the hem. The width of the fabric limits the width at the hemline.

3 Mark ½″–¾″ (1.3–1.9cm) seam allowances at the bottom opening.

4 Cut on the markings, but *do not cut the fabric fold*, to create 1 skirt front and 1 skirt back.

SEWING THE 5 BASIC STYLES

THIS CHAPTER DEMONSTRATES THE BASIC STEPS FOR SEWING THE FIVE BASIC STYLES: THE T-SHIRT/DRESS, SWEATER, TROUSERS, LEGGINGS, AND SKIRT. THE STYLEHACK PROJECT PAGES WILL REFER BACK TO THESE STEPS, SO IT IS A GOOD IDEA TO READ THEM HERE.

MANY STYLES ARE SEWN WITH THE SAME TECHNIQUES, SO EVEN THOUGH SOME VARIATIONS MIGHT NOT LOOK THE SAME, THEY ARE STITCHED IN THE SAME WAY. IF A SPECIFIC STYLE HAS A DIFFERENT, OR UNIQUE, SEWING TECHNIQUE, IT WILL BE DESCRIBED IN THAT STYLEHACK PROJECT'S INSTRUCTIONS.

Tip

Try on your styleHacked item when you have stitched it together and before you add the finishing touches. This way you can adjust the fit. When you are sure it fits, then you can add the finishing details.

Sewing T-Shirts, Tops, and Dresses

Use ½″ seam allowances unless otherwise noted.

1 Finish the cut edges with a zigzag stitch or serge them so they do not fray.

2 Pin or clip the front piece and back piece with right sides together.

3 Sew the pieces together with a straight stitch along the shoulders and underarms.

4 Finish the neckline, sleeve openings, and hems as desired (see Hemming, page 19, and Edge Finishes, page 21).

Tip

I always mark and cut the neck opening so it is on the small side and then try on the stitched garment. This way you can cut a bit more to make it wider and more open if you prefer.

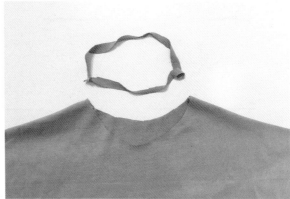

Sewing Sweaters and Garments with Sleeves

Use ½″ seam allowances unless otherwise noted.

1 Finish the cut edges with a zigzag stitch or serge them so they do not fray.

2 Pin or clip the front piece and back piece with right sides together.

3 Sew the pieces together along the shoulders using a straight stitch.

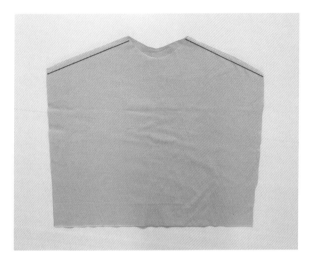

4 Match the center of the sleeve with the shoulder seam. Pin or clip the sleeve to the side opening with right sides together.

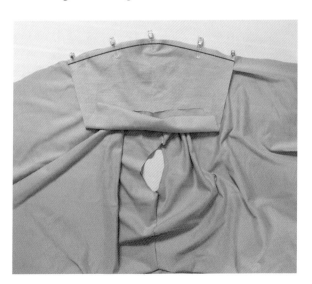

If the sleeve template had a pointed edge, curve the fabric pieces slightly before stitching to the side opening.

5 Stitch the sleeve seam with a straight stitch or zigzag stitch, or use a serger.

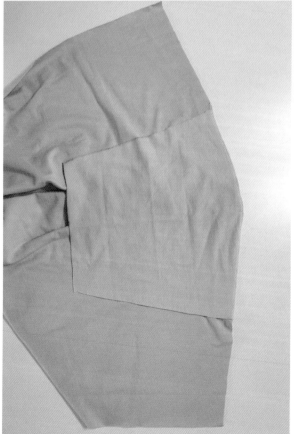

THIS CHAPTER DEMONSTRATES THE BASIC STEPS FOR SEWING THE FIVE BASIC STYLES: THE T-SHIRT/DRESS, SWEATER, TROUSERS, LEGGINGS, AND SKIRT. THE STYLEHACK PROJECT PAGES WILL REFER BACK TO THESE STEPS, SO IT IS A GOOD IDEA TO READ THEM HERE.

MANY STYLES ARE SEWN WITH THE SAME TECHNIQUES, SO EVEN THOUGH SOME VARIATIONS MIGHT NOT LOOK THE SAME, THEY ARE STITCHED IN THE SAME WAY. IF A SPECIFIC STYLE HAS A DIFFERENT, OR UNIQUE, SEWING TECHNIQUE, IT WILL BE DESCRIBED IN THAT STYLEHACK PROJECT'S INSTRUCTIONS.

Tip

Try on your styleHacked item when you have stitched it together and before you add the finishing touches. This way you can adjust the fit. When you are sure it fits, then you can add the finishing details.

Sewing T-Shirts, Tops, and Dresses

Use ½˝ seam allowances unless otherwise noted.

1 Finish the cut edges with a zigzag stitch or serge them so they do not fray.

2 Pin or clip the front piece and back piece with right sides together.

3 Sew the pieces together with a straight stitch along the shoulders and underarms.

4 Finish the neckline, sleeve openings, and hems as desired (see Hemming, page 19, and Edge Finishes, page 21).

Tip

I always mark and cut the neck opening so it is on the small side and then try on the stitched garment. This way you can cut a bit more to make it wider and more open if you prefer.

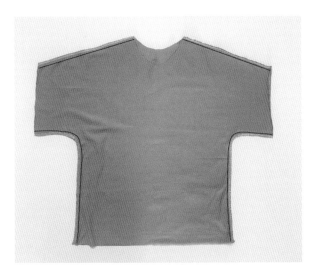

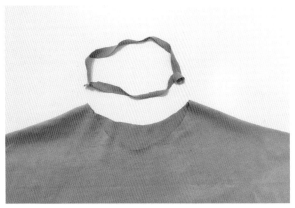

Sewing Trousers and Leggings

Use ½˝ seam allowances unless otherwise noted.

1 Finish the cut edges with a zigzag stitch or serge them so they do not fray.

2 Pin or clip the 2 front pieces with right sides together along the center front seam. Pin or clip the 2 back pieces with right sides together along the center back seam.

3 Sew the front pieces together with a straight stitch. Repeat for the back pieces.

4 Align the front and back center seams with right sides together. Using a straight stitch and starting at the center seam, sew the pieces together down the inner seam of one of the legs. Then begin at the center seam again and sew down the inner seam of the other leg.

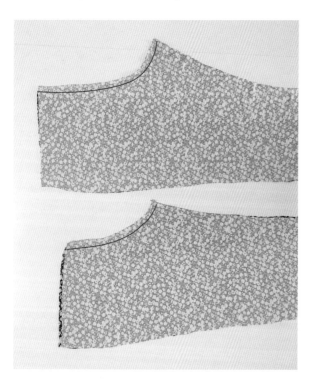

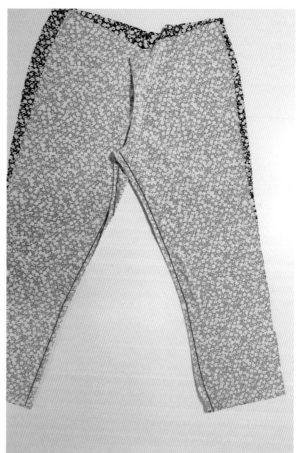

5 Sew the side seams with right sides together. Try on the garment at this stage so see if you need to make any size adjustments.

6 Finish the waist and leg openings as desired (see Hemming, page 19, and Edge Finishes, page 21).

Sewing Skirts

Use ½˝ seam allowances unless otherwise noted.

1 Finish the cut edges with a zigzag stitch or serge them so they do not fray.

2 Pin or clip the front piece and back piece with right sides together.

3 Sew the pieces together with a straight stitch along side seams, from the waist to the hem. Try on the skirt at this stage to see if you need to make any fit adjustments.

4 Finish the waist edges and hems as desired (see Hemming, page 19, and Edge Finishes, page 21).

Styles to *Hack*

It's time to have some fun! Now you can put your newly found knowledge about basic styleHacking and different finishing techniques to the test. You've already learned the principles of marking, cutting, and sewing, so you can hack all the designs and styles that you can imagine.

The following pages are meant to inspire you as you see how to use the templates to many great styles, many of which are shown with several design variations.

A few tips to get you started:

• Standard seam allowance is ½″–¾″ (1.3–1.9cm). For many of the styles, the seam allowance is the same around all the edges. On others, however, you might want to allow extra seam allowance for fit and experimentation. An extra seam allowance of 2″ (5cm) is a good amount to start, but you can always make it wider if you find the extra seam allowance suits your styleHacking skills.

- Finish all the cut edges with a zigzag stitch or serger so they do not fray before you begin to sew the pieces together.

- Try on the project once you have stitched it together but before you add the finishing touches. This allows you to adjust the fit or design details before you finish sewing it. This is not trial and error—this is try and adjust!

- Refer to the illustrations as you mark and cut for your own styles. Do not worry about small measurement variances, like whether you need to sew ½″ or 1″ or 5″ or 6″. In this way you can create garments with a sense of freedom because there is no wrong or right way to do it. You just need to be able to fit into your projects using the smallest of seam allowances. This will happen if you made your templates correctly.

- The styleHacking projects will not have a lot of instructional steps. The instructions are meant to be visual and inspiring, and to show you how to make lines around your templates to create new styles. You already know how to sew the fabric pieces together from the technique pages (see Sewing the 5 Basic Styles, page 46).

- With practice, you can begin to know how much fabric you need and what type of style changes you want to make to the templates by deciding if you want your finished style to be loose, tight, long, or short. Or perhaps look at the fabrics you own and start to wonder what you can make with them.

I wish you the best of luck! I'm sure you will have lots of fun and make some amazing styleHacks that are perfect for you.

BASIC T-SHIRT
Shown with A-Line Skirt (page 74)

Marking and Cutting the Fabric

Suggested fabrics: Jersey or other stretch fabric

1 Use the T-shirt template. Fold the bottom corner of the sleeve template up so it is easier to draw the underarm curve.

2 Mark ½″–¾″ (1.3–1.9cm) seam allowances on the neck, side, and bottom edges. Adjust the markings from the shoulder seam and around the sleeve for a wider sleeve opening, as shown. With these adjustments, the marked sleeve opening should be larger than the sleeve opening of the actual T-shirt template.

3 Fold, mark, and cut the fabric to make 1 front and 1 back, both cut on the fabric fold.

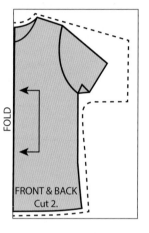

 Tip

For a looser-fitting T-shirt, elongate the sleeve and make the seam allowance wider from the shoulder, down the sleeve opening, and through to the hem.

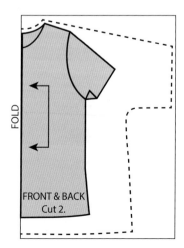

Sewing

1 Sew the pieces together (see Sewing T-Shirts, Tops, and Dresses, page 47). Try on the garment and make any fit or design adjustments before finishing the edges.

2 Finish the neckline, sleeve openings, and hemline as desired (see Hemming, page 19, and Edge Finishes, page 21).

Tip

There are several ways to finish these T-shirts. Your fabric selection and finishing technique can make the T-shirt very casual, business appropriate, or even suitable for a more formal event. You can make it any length: cropped, hip length, or even longer!

BASIC T-SHIRT WITH FABRIC BANDS

Shown with a variety of basic trousers

Marking and Cutting the Fabric

Suggested fabrics: Jersey or other stretch fabric

1 Use the T-shirt template. The neck, sleeves, and bottom hem are finished with fabric bands. Decide on the size for the fabric bands. You can experiment with how wide you want the bands; I like ½″ (1.3cm)-wide bands. Subtract the width from the desired size of the neck opening and the length of the sleeves and T-shirt.

2 Use this formula for the cut sizes of the fabric bands:

Length: The same length (or slightly shorter) than the opening measurements plus 2 times the seam allowance

Width: 2 times the desired height plus 2 times the seam allowance

3 Place the T-shirt template on the fabric. Fold the bottom corner of the sleeve template up so it easier to draw the underarm curve. Add ½″–¾″ (1.3–1.9cm) seam allowances unless otherwise noted.

4 Fold, mark, and cut the fabric to make 1 front and 1 back, both cut on the fabric fold. Also cut 1 neckband and 1 hem band, both cut on the fold, and 2 sleeve bands.

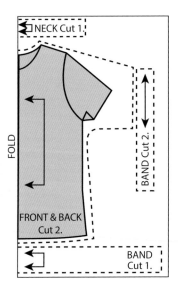

A quick and easy alternative is to simply hem the sleeves and the bottom of the T-shirt.

VARIATION

For a looser fit, make the following adjustments before cutting the fabric: Make the sleeves longer and wider, and add extra seam allowance along the side seam.

Sewing

1 Sew the pieces together (see Sewing T-Shirts, Tops, and Dresses, page 47). Try on the garment and make any fit or design adjustments before finishing the edges.

2 Prepare and sew the fabric bands to the neck, sleeve, and hem edges (see Fabric Bands, page 24).

BASIC T-SHIRT WITH RUFFLES

Shown with a variety of basic trousers

Marking and Cutting the Fabric

Fabric suggestions: Jersey and other stretch fabric

1 Use the basic T-shirt template.

2 Decide how long you want the finished T-shirt. You can then shorten or lengthen the template by determining the width of the ruffle.

3 Use these formulas for the adjustments to the pieces and the cut size of the ruffles:

For a hemline ruffle: Shorten the T-shirt front and back by the width of the ruffle plus the seam allowance.

For a sleeve ruffle: Shorten the sleeves by the width of the ruffle plus the seam allowance.

Ruffle width: Desired width plus 2 times the seam allowance

Ruffle length: 1–2 times longer than the bottom opening (or sleeve hem opening)

4 Fold, mark, and cut the fabric to make 1 front, 1 back, and 2 ruffles, all cut on the fabric fold.

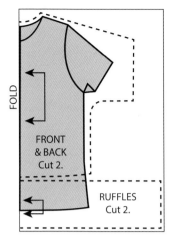

Make the sleeves wider and shape the side seam near the hemline.

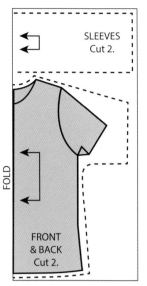

This T-shirt features sleeve ruffles. Mark the sleeves wider than the template.

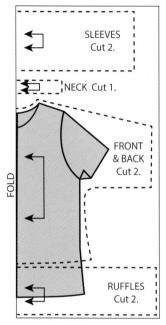

This lace T-shirt features a hemline ruffle, sleeve ruffle, and fabric neck-band.

Sewing

1 Sew the pieces together (see Sewing T-Shirts, Tops, and Dresses, page 47).

2 Finish the neckline with a fabric band or one of the edge finishes (see Edge Finishes, page 21).

3 Prepare and sew the ruffles to the edges (see Making Ruffles, page 30).

4 For any edges not finished with a ruffle, use a double-fold or other hem (see Hemming, page 19).

WOVEN FABRIC TOPS

Shown with Basic Trousers (page 86)

Marking and Cutting the Fabric

Suggested fabrics: Lightweight woven cotton, viscose, or silk fabrics

1 Use the T-shirt template. Fold the bottom corner of the sleeve up so it easier to draw the underarm curve. These tops, like the T-shirt, have sleeves that are a continuation of the front and back pieces instead of separate pieces.

2 Fold, mark, and cut the fabric to make 1 front and 1 back piece. Since this top is made with woven fabrics, you need to add at least 2″ extra seam allowance along the sleeve and side seams. For a looser fit, add more width to the seam allowances. Use the standard ½″–¾″ (1.3–1.9cm) seam allowance for the neckline and shoulders.

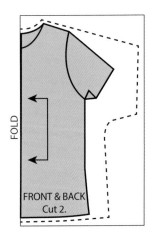

FOLD

FRONT & BACK
Cut 2.

Sewing

1 Sew the pieces together (see Sewing T-Shirts, Tops, and Dresses, page 47).

2 It is important to try on the top before finishing the neck to make sure it pulls comfortably over your head. You can make it wider and more open if needed.

Tip: Adjusting Necklines

I always cut my necklines quite small so they do not suddenly get too wide, especially if the fabric stretches. Once the top or dress is sewn together, I try it on and look at the neckline in the mirror so I can see more clearly the best way to adjust it. I might like a wide boat neckline; a small, narrow neckline; or even a deeper neckline. Most often, the back neckline is fine as it is, but sometimes I alter it slightly so it fits the front neck opening at the shoulders. *Never cut the marked front neckline opening on the back of the garment.*

While you have the garment on, decide how you want to adjust your neckline. Mark right on the front of the top or dress with pins, tailor's chalk, or washable fabric markers exactly where you want the opening to be.

Take off the garment and adjust the design line markings so the neckline it is symmetrical, and then *add the seam allowance*—you don't want to cut the fabric at the design line.

Cut along the marked seam allowance to create a new neckline.

3 Finish the neckline, sleeves, and bottom hem. The sleeves and the bottom hem can be finished differently, not necessarily in the same way that the neckline is finished. For instance, the neckline on this top is finished with bias tape (see Bias Tape, page 21). The sleeves and bottom feature a single-fold hem (see Hemming, page 19).

Variations

There are so many ways to add your own design style to this simple top. Here are few suggestions!

• Mark the sleeves at the desired length or make them as long as the fabric allows.

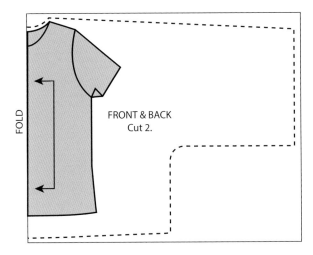

• Turn the top into a dress by making it longer. Keep the boxy shape by extending the side seam straight down to the hemline. Or make an A-line shape and curve the bottom hemline slightly as it nears the side seam.

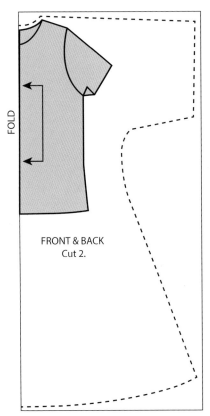

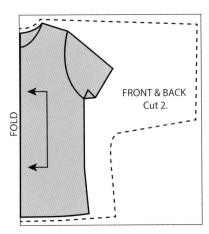

• Add more seam allowance at the sides and under the arm (since you are using a template made from a stretchy style for a style made in woven fabric). An extra seam allowance of 2″ (5cm) is a good start, but you can add more for a boxier and looser look and fit. Use the standard seam allowance of ½″–¾″ (1.3–1.9cm) for the neckline and hems.

• Just look at what you can create with a novelty print fabric! Carefully mark the cutting lines to best showcase a motif or favorite part of your fabric.

BOX-SHAPED TOP WITH SLEEVE VARIATIONS

Marking and Cutting the Fabric

Suggested fabrics: Lightweight woven cotton, viscose, or silk

For both sleeve variations:

• Use the T-shirt template. Fold the bottom corner of the sleeve template up so it easier to draw the underarm curve.

• Add a ½″–¾″ (1.3–1.9cm) seam allowance unless otherwise noted.

• Mark and cut the neck opening so it is on the small side. This way you can make it wider and more open once you sew the front and back pieces together.

BOX-SHAPED TOP WITH SEPARATE SLEEVES

1 Make the style markings as follows:

Back: Mark the new shoulder and side seams to create a boxier design; an extra seam allowance of at least 2″ (5cm) is a good start. This is particularly important when you use woven fabric. Make the back (and front) as short or long as you want or however long the fabric allows it to be. Curve the bottom line as shown.

Front: Use the new pattern for the back to mark the front, remembering to trace the front neckline.

Sleeves: Measure the distance from the new shoulder line to the underarm, indicated by point B. Use that measurement to draw a rectangle that is 2 times the measurement of A plus 2 times the seam allowance by the desired length of the sleeves plus 2 times the seam allowance. For a looser fit, make measurement A longer than the actual measurement.

2 Fold, mark, and cut the fabric to make 1 back and 1 front, both cut on the fabric fold, and 2 sleeves.

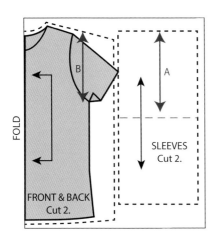

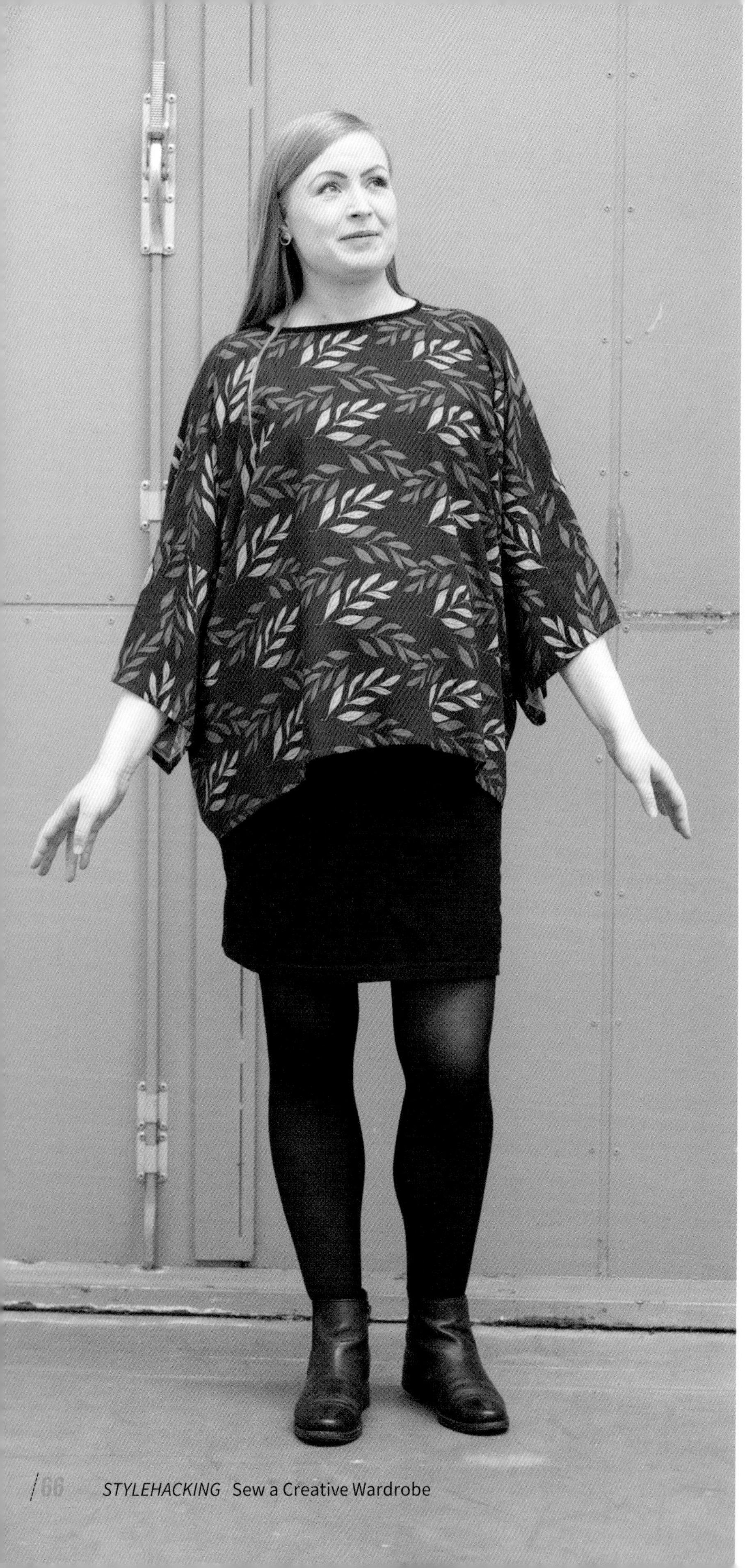

BOX-SHAPED TOP WITH INTEGRATED SLEEVES

1 Make the style markings as follows:

Back: Mark a new shoulder cutting line extending straight out from the neckline and shoulder point as far as the width of the fabric allows. Use a ruler to draw the sleeve hem, underarm seam, and side seam. Make a small curve under the arm, where the lines meet, instead of a 90° angle. The side seam should be at least 2˝ (5cm) wider than the template side seam, as shown. Make the back (and front) as short or long as you want or however long the fabric allows it to be. Curve the bottom line as shown. Use the standard seam allowance of ½˝–¾˝ (1.3–1.9cm) for the neckline and hems.

Front: Use the new pattern for the back to mark the front, remembering to trace the front neckline.

2 Fold, mark, and cut the fabric to make 1 back and 1 front, both cut on the fabric fold.

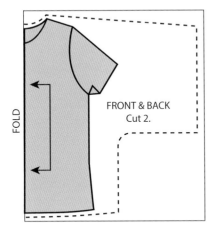

FRONT & BACK
Cut 2.

FOLD

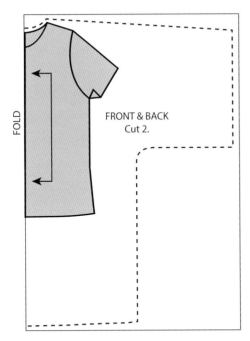

FRONT & BACK
Cut 2.

FOLD

Sewing

1 **Variation with separate sleeves:** Sew the pieces together (see Sewing Sweaters and Garments with Sleeves, page 48). Note that although these sleeves are rectangular, they are sewn on the same way.

Variation with integrated sleeves: Sew the pieces together (see Sewing T-Shirts, Tops, and Dresses, page 47).

2 Before finishing the hems and openings, try on the garment to see if you need to sew it a bit smaller or make other fit adjustments.

3 Finish the neckline with bias tape (see Bias Tape, page 21). Hem the bottom opening and the sleeve openings as desired (see Hemming, page 19).

TUBE TOP

Shown with A-Line Skirt (page 74)

Marking and Cutting the Fabric

Fabric suggestions: Jersey and other stretch fabric

1 Use the tank top template. Adapt the template for a tube top and determine the size for the fabric band (see Using the Tank Top Template to Cut a Tube Top, page 34).

2 Fold, mark, and cut the fabric to make 1 front and 1 back, both cut on the fabric fold, and 1 fabric band. Use the standard seam allowance of ½″–¾″ (1.3–1.9cm).

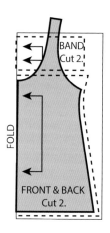

Tip

The fabric band piece can be cut in 2 shorter lengths and stitched together.

Sewing

1 Sew the side seams with right sides together.

2 Attach the fabric band (see Fabric Bands with Elastic, page 25).

3 Hem the bottom edge using a single- or double-fold hem (see Hemming, page 19).

WRAP TOP

Shown with A-Line Skirt with Slits (page 78)

Marking and Cutting the Fabric

This top can be worn with the wrap toward the front or the back.

Fabric suggestions: Lightweight woven cotton, viscose, or silk fabrics

1 Use the T-shirt template. Fold the bottom corner of the sleeve template up so it easier to draw the underarm curve. You will also need a T-shirt full template (see Making a Full Template, page 32).

2 Make the style markings as follows:

• For both the front and back, mark the sleeves at the desired length or make them as long as the fabric allows.

• Add extra seam allowance to the sides and under the arm. Add 2″ (5cm) since the template was made for stretch fabrics. Add more than 2″ (5cm) for a boxier and looser look and fit. Use the standard seam allowance of ½″–¾″ (1.3–1.9cm) for the neckline, sleeve openings, and bottom edges.

Back: Trace the T-shirt half-template along the fabric fold. Follow the back neck cutting line.

Front: Position the T-shirt full template on 2 layers of fabric with right sides together. Center the template so you can mark the same sleeve length as the back. Mark the shoulder, arm, and side seams of the right edge of the template, matching the back piece.

As you mark the bottom of the T-shirt front to match the T-shirt back, extend the cutting line past the left side of the template for about 8˝ (20cm), gently curving it upward, as shown.

Use a ruler to mark a diagonal line from the neck opening at the right shoulder point through the left side seam, slightly below the underarm seam, and continuing to 2˝ (5cm) above the bottom hem marking on the left side. Draw a straight line from the end of the diagonal line to the extended hem marking.

Bands: Measure around your body to determine the lengths for the tie bands. They should be long enough so you can tie them in a bow or square knot. Mark 2 bands, each 2˝ wide by the length to wrap around your body and tie comfortably.

3 Mark and cut 1 back piece on the fabric fold, 2 front pieces, and 2 band pieces.

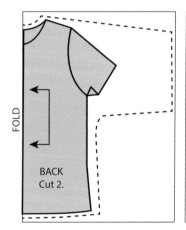

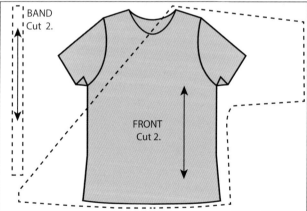

Sewing

1 Pin or clip the front pieces to the back piece with right sides together and the overlap in position. Stitch the upper sleeve seams first, from the neck edge to the ends of the sleeves.

2 With right sides together, sew the underarm seams, starting at the sleeve opening.

3 With right sides together, sew one narrow end of each band to the straight edge near the hemline of each extended front piece.

4 Try on the garment and make any fit or design adjustments before finishing the edges.

5 Finish all the edges, including the bottom hem, with a narrow single-fold or double-fold hem (see Hemming, page 19).

FAUX WRAP TOP

Shown with A-Line Skirt with Tiers (page 79)

Marking and Cutting the Fabric

This top can be worn with the wrap on the front or the back. These steps show the wrap on the back.

Suggested fabrics: Jersey or other stretch fabric

1 Use the T-shirt template. Fold the bottom corner of the sleeve template up so it easier to draw the underarm curve. You will also need a T-shirt full template (see Making a Full Template, page 32).

2 Make the style markings as follows:

- For both the front and back, mark the sleeves at the desired length or make them as long as the fabric allows.

- Add extra seam allowance under the arm for a wide kimono style; 2″ (5cm) is a good start. Use the standard seam allowance of ½″–¾″ (1.3–1.9cm) for the neckline, sleeve opening, and bottom edges.

- Mark both the front and back pieces a bit shorter than the T-shirt template so the finished top is a bit more cropped. Make the bottom line a slight curve, as shown.

Front: Mark the half-template along the fabric fold, as shown. Follow the front neck cutting line.

Back: Position the full template on 2 layers of fabric. Center the template so you can mark the same sleeve length and bottom hemline as for the front piece. Use a ruler to mark a diagonal line from the shoulder point at the neck opening to 2″ (5cm) above the bottom hem marking on the opposite side seam.

3 Mark and cut 1 front piece on the fabric fold and 2 back pieces.

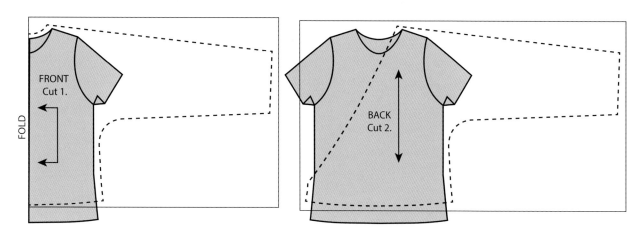

Sewing

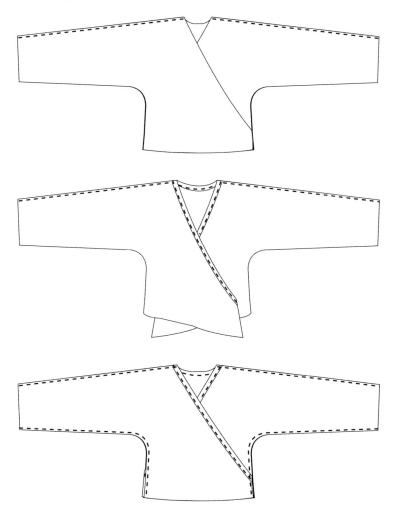

1 Pin or clip the back pieces over the front piece with right sides together and the overlap in position. Stitch the upper sleeve seams first, from the neck edge to the bottom edge of the sleeves.

2 Finish the neck and overlap edges with a narrow hem (see Hemming, page 19).

3 Pin or clip the underarm and side seams, including the overlap edges in the side seams. Stitch the seams, starting at the sleeve opening.

4 Hem the sleeve openings and the bottom with the same finishing method as the neck and overlap edges.

A-LINE SKIRT

Shown with Basic T-Shirt (page 54) and
Tube Top (page 68)

Marking and Cutting the Fabric

Any type of fabric is suitable. The width of the fabric
determines the fullness of the skirt.

1 Use the trousers back template to mark both the
  skirt front and back.

2 Make the style markings as follows:

• Place the side seam of the template on the fold of
  the fabric, with the highest part of the template,
  point A, about 1″ (2.5cm) from the top edge of the
  fabric. If you plan to finish the waist with an elastic
  casing, place the template about 4″ (10.1cm) from
  the top edge.

• Use a ruler to draw a line from the inseam, point B,
  to the top edge of the fabric.

• Measure ½″–¾″ (1.3–1.9cm) above point A, and
  draw a line from the fabric fold to intersect with
  the previous line. This becomes point C.

• Point C indicates the point where the waist and
  side seam meet. To check that the waistline will
  be wide enough, measure from the fabric fold
  to point C. That measurement times 4 minus
  approximately 2″ (5cm) for seam allowance is the
  finished waist measurement. If you wish to reduce
  or enlarge the waistline, redraw the point B and C
  lines accordingly. When you enlarge the waistline,
  there will be more gathers in the skirt.

• Draw a line for the side seam from point C toward
  the fabric selvages to make the skirt as long and
  as full (wide) as you would like.

• Draw the bottom edge, allowing for a 1″–2″ (2.5–5cm) hem, curving the line slightly as it nears the side seamline.

VARIATION

For a fuller, looser style, add a wider seam allowance. You can also make the skirt as long or short as you would like.

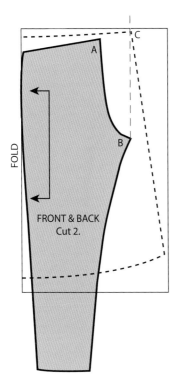

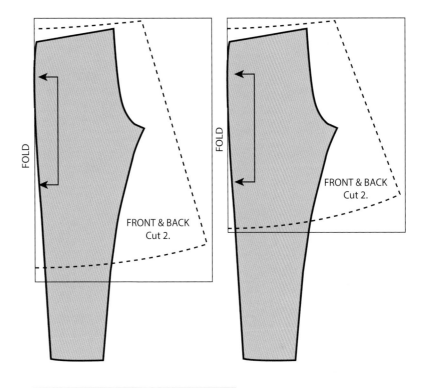

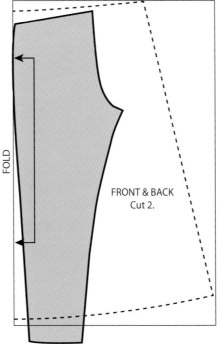

3 Make adjustments to the waist if needed for the desired waist finish (see Elastic Casing, page 28).

4 Fold, mark, and cut the fabric to make 1 skirt front and 1 skirt back, both cut on the fabric fold.

Sewing

1 Pin or clip the front piece and back piece with right sides together. Sew the side seams (see Sewing Skirts, page 51).

2 Finish the waist opening using your choice of finishes (see Edge Finishes, page 21).

3 Hem the skirt using your choice of hem (see Hemming, page 19).

Sewing a Decorative Elastic Waist Finish

Finish the waist opening with decorative elastic; a contrasting elastic band will add design interest (see Decorative Elastic, page 27).

Note: If you have marked and cut the waist opening extra wide, you will need to first gather the skirt to fit the decorative elastic, since it is cut to your waist measurement (see Gathering Fabric, page 29).

VARIATION

Using a fabric with a bordered edge, like this scalloped-edge lace, turns a basic A-line skirt into a simple, elegant style. To use a bordered edge, you'll need to mark the skirt so that the bottom of the skirt is along the decorative edge. Wear it with a stretch rayon or silk fabric T-shirt to dress up this style nicely.

Sewing an Elastic Casing Waist Finish

1 Measure the width of the elastic you plan to use (⅝″–1″ is fairly standard). Calculate 2 times the width of the elastic plus the seam allowance of ½″–¾″ (1.3–1.9cm). Using this measurement, extend the side seam at the waist while marking the skirt. This is best used on skirts that are straighter and boxier than the basic A-line shape.

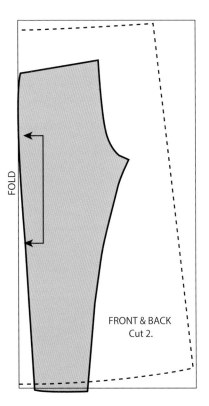

FOLD

FRONT & BACK
Cut 2.

2 Finish the waist opening with an elastic casing (see Elastic Casing, page 28).

A-LINE SKIRT WITH SLITS

Shown with Wrap Top (page 69)

Marking and Cutting the Fabric

Fabric suggestions: Light-weight cotton, viscose, or silk

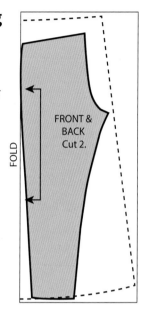

1 Use the trousers back template.

2 Mark and cut 1 skirt front and 1 skirt back (see A-Line Skirt, Marking and Cutting the Fabric, page 74).

Sewing

1 Determine how long you want the slits and mark the fabric. Pin the skirt back and skirt front with right sides together. Sew the side seams to the marks; backstitch at the end of the seam.

2 Fold and press the open edges of the side seams toward the wrong side.

3 Stitch close to the pressed edges.

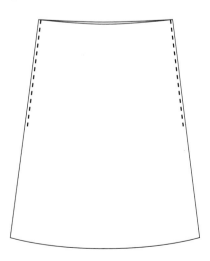

4 Fold and press the bottom edge ½″–¾″ (1.3–1.9cm) to the wrong side. Stitch close to the fold to hem the skirt.

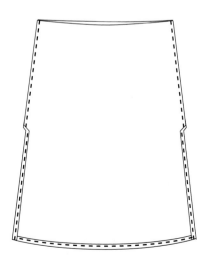

A-LINE SKIRT WITH TIERS

Shown with Faux Wrap Top (page 72)

Marking and Cutting the Fabric

Fabric suggestions: Lightweight cotton, viscose, or silk

1 Use the trousers back template.

2 Mark and cut 1 skirt front and 1 skirt back (see A-Line Skirt, Marking and Cutting the Fabric, page 74).

3 From a separate piece of fabric, cut the tiers. Follow the instructions for tier sizes in Making a Tiered Skirt (page 31).

4 This skirt has 2 tiers but requires 6 rectangles of fabric because 2 rectangles are used to create the first tier and 4 rectangles are used to create the second tier. Measure and cut 6 tier pieces on the crosswise fabric fold.

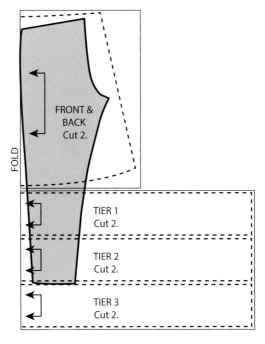

FOLD

FRONT & BACK Cut 2.

TIER 1 Cut 2.

TIER 2 Cut 2.

TIER 3 Cut 2.

Sewing

1 Sew the ends of 2 rectangle pieces right sides together to make the first tier. Sew the 4 remaining rectangular pieces right sides together; then join the ends to make the second tier.

2 Pin or clip the front piece and back piece with right sides together. Sew the side seams (see Sewing Skirts, page 51).

3 Finish the waist opening using your choice of finishes (see Edge Finishes, page 21).

4 Gather the first tier and sew to the skirt bottom edge. Gather the second tier and sew to the bottom of the first tier (see Gathering Fabric, page 29).

5 Use a narrow hem to finish the bottom edge of the second tier (see Hemming, page 19).

TUBE SKIRT

Shown with Box-Shaped Top with Sleeve Variations (page 64)

Marking and Cutting the Fabric

Fabric suggestions: Jersey or other stretch fabric

1 Use the trousers back template. Place the template so the side seam is along the fabric fold, and mark a square around the outline of the template as shown. Mark and cut the fabric to make 1 front and 1 back, both cut on the fabric fold. Use the standard seam allowance of ½″–¾″ (1.3–1.9cm).

2 Mark the rectangular piece for the waistband casing. The width should be 2 times the desired width plus 2 times the seam allowance. The length should be ½″–1″ (1.3–2.5cm) smaller than the waist width of the skirt pieces once sewn or your waist measurement.

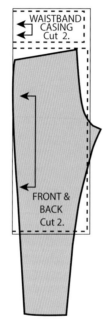

Sewing

1 Pin or clip the front piece and back piece with right sides together. Sew the side seams (see Sewing Skirts, page 51).

2 Finish the waist opening with the fabric band (see Fabric Bands with Elastic, page 25).

3 Use a zigzag hem finish on the bottom opening (see Zigzag Edge, page 20).

CIRCLE SKIRT

Marking and Cutting the Fabric

Suggested fabrics: Fabrics without directional designs

1 Use the trousers back template.

2 Fold the fabric in half lengthwise; then fold again to make 4 layers, with folds on the side and at the top. Position the template diagonally on the folded fabric, as shown. You will only need to mark 1 skirt piece.

3 Make the style markings as follows:

• Measure the width of the template's top edge. Use that measurement to mark a waistline curve between the folded edges.

• Decide how long you want the skirt. Measure from the waistline curve, down one side of the folded fabric, to mark the desired skirt length plus the seam allowance. The skirt can be as short as you wish or as long as the available amount of fabric.

• Mark the same measurement from the waistline to the hemline in several places to provide guides to draw the hemline curve. Connect the markings to draw the hemline curve.

4 Cut the fabric on the marked lines to make 1 skirt. Unfold the fabric; it will be a circular shape with a circular opening in the middle. Try the skirt on and make any necessary adjustments to the waist.

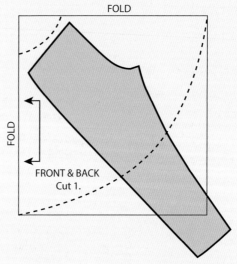

FOLD

FOLD

FRONT & BACK
Cut 1.

Sewing

1 Finish the waist edge with your choice of technique (see Edge Finishes, page 21). The models are wearing circle skirts that feature a wide contrasting fabric band (see Fabric Bands with Elastic, page 25).

Note: If the waist opening is considerably larger than the fabric band, gather the waist to fit the band (see Gathering Fabric, page 29).

2 Use a narrow hem finish because of the volume of the fabric (see Hemming, page 19).

FAUX WRAP RUFFLE SKIRT

Shown with Kimono Top (page 116)

Marking and Cutting the Fabric

Fabric suggestions: Woven fabric with a soft drape, like cotton, viscose, or silk

1 Use the trousers back template. Decide on the length of the skirt and the size of the ruffles. Deduct the size of the ruffles from the length of the skirt to calculate what length to cut the skirt pieces. *Note:* In this example, the skirt features ruffles cut 5″ (12.7cm) wide.

2 Mark and cut 1 skirt front and 1 skirt back (see A-Line Skirt, Marking and Cutting the Fabric, page 74). Also cut an additional skirt front piece that is narrower by the same amount as the ruffle width. In this example, the additional skirt front piece was cut 5″ (12.7cm) narrower. Cut a curve in the second skirt front piece.

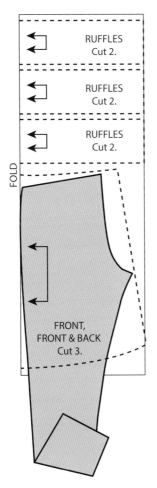

3 From a separate piece of fabric, cut the 3 rectangles, each the width of the fabric by the desired ruffle size.

Sewing

1 Pin or clip the front pieces to the back piece with right sides together. Sew the pieces together as shown.

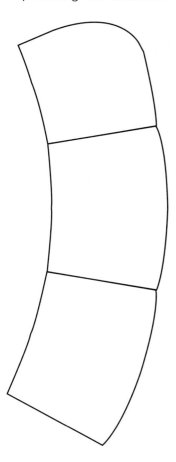

2 The ruffle should be 2–3 times longer than the bottom edge and curved front edge. Measure the sewn skirt and make any adjustments. Sew the ruffle rectangles with right sides together to make 1 long ruffle piece.

3 Gather one raw edge of the ruffle piece to fit the bottom and curved edge of the skirt pieces (see Gathering Fabric, page 29).

Pin or clip the ruffle to the skirt, starting at the top of the curve and ending at the bottom corner, as shown. Sew the ruffle in place, adjusting the gathers to keep them evenly distributed.

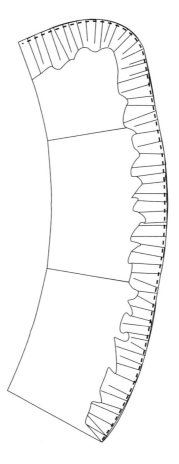

4 Use a narrow hem finish for the other edge of the ruffle to finish the edges (see Hemming, page 19).

5 Lay out the skirt so the edge of the ruffle on the curved wrap meets the side seam, as shown. Pin or clip the wrap in place and baste the edges together.

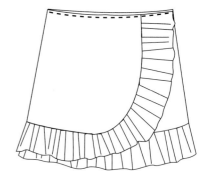

6 From 2″ (5cm)-wide decorative elastic, cut your waist measurement plus 1″ (2.5cm).

7 Gather the top edge of the skirt as needed and attach the elastic (see Decorative Elastic, page 27).

FAUX WRAP BOX SKIRT

Shown with Kimono Top (page 116)

Marking and Cutting the Fabric

Fabric suggestions: Woven fabric with a soft drape

1 This style is super simple; it is basically just one big piece of fabric. Make the style markings as follows:

Length: Desired finished length plus 2 times the standard seam allowance ½″–¾″ (1.3–1.9cm).

Width: Wrap the fabric around the widest part of your hips, extending it as far past your center front as you wish for the overlap. Mark the fabric at the point you want the overlap to stop plus 2 times the standard seam allowance ½″–¾″ (1.3–1.9cm).

2 Mark and cut 1 skirt piece.

Sewing

1 Hem both side edges and the bottom edge of the skirt piece (see Hemming, page 19).

2 Arrange the skirt piece so the overlap is in the correct position, and pin the front layers together. Baste the top edge to make it easier to attach the decorative elastic.

3 From 2″ (5cm)-wide decorative elastic, cut your waist measurement plus 1″ (2.5cm).

4 Gather the top edge of the skirt as needed and attach the elastic (see Decorative Elastic, page 27).

BASIC TROUSERS

Shown with Woven Fabric Top (page 60)

Marking and Cutting the Fabric

Suggested fabrics: Woven cotton or viscose. For loose, stretchy trousers, use jersey or other stretch fabrics.

1 Use the trousers front and back templates to make several variations of a basic pair of pull-on trousers. Mark the changes to make a variety of styles.

2 Add the standard seam allowance of ½″–¾″ (1.3–1.9cm) on all the edges except the legs, where you can add varying widths of seam allowance according to how wide or how flared or long or short you want the legs.

3 Cut 2 trousers front pieces and 2 trousers back pieces.

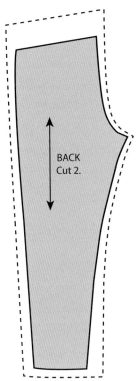

BACK
Cut 2.

For basic trousers, straighten the leg as shown and add extra height at the waistline for an elastic casing (see Elastic Casing, page 28).

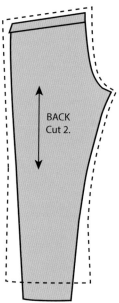

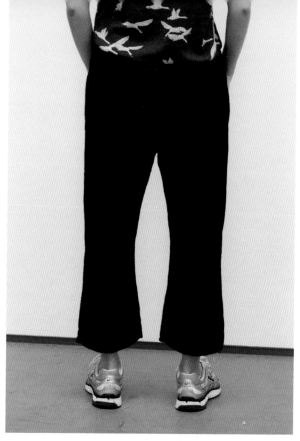

Starting at the knee area, flare out on both sides of the leg template. Crop the length as desired.

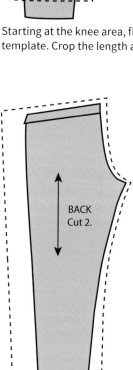

To use decorative elastic to finish the waistline, fold down the waist the same amount as the width of the elastic minus the seam allowance. You can add the same elastic at the leg hems (see Decorative Elastic, page 27). A casing for elastic will also control the fullness at the ankles (see Elastic Casing, page 28). You can add extra width at the side seams to create a fuller leg; start with 2″ (5cm).

Sewing

1 Sew the trouser pieces together (see Sewing Trousers and Leggings, page 50).

2 Finish the waist opening with your choice of finishes (see Edge Finishes, page 21). For trousers made from stretch fabrics, finish the waist opening with a fabric band in the same fabric (see Fabric Bands with Elastic, page 25).

3 Hem the trousers using your choice of hem (see Hemming, page 19).

LEGGINGS AND BIKE SHORTS

Shown with a variety of sweater tops

Marking and Cutting the Fabric

Fabric suggestions: Jersey and other stretch fabric

1 Use the leggings template.

2 Cut the length as desired for full-length leggings, capri-length leggings, or bike shorts. Add the standard seam allowance of ½″–¾″ (1.3–1.9cm) to all edges.

3 Fold, mark, and cut the fabric to make 2 leggings front pieces and 2 leggings back pieces.

4 Vary the waistline finishes as desired.

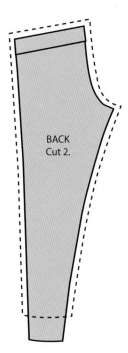

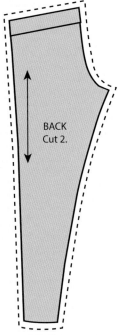

To add a decorative elastic band, fold down the height of the elastic at the waistline minus the seam allowance.

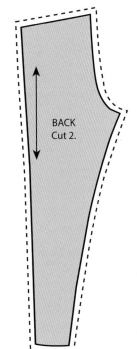

For a high-waist version, maintain the template waistline and add decorative elastic to the top of the waist.

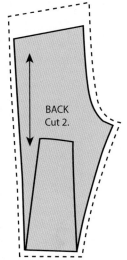

To create an elastic casing, add extra fabric at the top of the waist.

Sewing

1 Sew the pieces together (see Sewing Trousers and Leggings, page 50).

2 Finish the edges with your choice of finishes (see Edge Finishes, page 21).

3 Hem the leg openings using your choice of hems (see Hemming, page 19). A zigzag stitch is an easy edge finish.

STRETCH JUMPSUIT

Marking and Cutting the Fabric

Fabric suggestions: Jersey and other stretch fabric

1 Use the leggings template and tank top template.

2 Try on the leggings and tank top that you used to make the templates and see how much they overlap at the waist. They can overlap a bit for a baggy effect.

3 Make the style markings as follows:

Front and back jumpsuit: You'll need 2 copies of the tank top template to pair with the leggings front and back templates. Position the templates as shown, overlapping the tank top hem and leggings waist the desired overlap amount.

Straps: Extend the tank top straps about 10˝ (25.4cm) or more, so you can tie them at your shoulders.

Fabric bands: Mark 4 rectangles 2˝ × 35˝ (5cm × 89cm) for the fabric bands to finish the armhole, strap, and neck edges.

4 From a double layer of fabric, mark and cut 2 jumpsuit fronts and 2 jumpsuit backs. Use the standard seam allowance of ½˝–¾˝ (1.3–1.9cm) on all the edges except the sides of the tank top. Make those side seam allowances 2˝ (5cm) to make sure you can get the jumpsuit on over your hips.

5 From a single layer of fabric, cut 4 fabric bands.

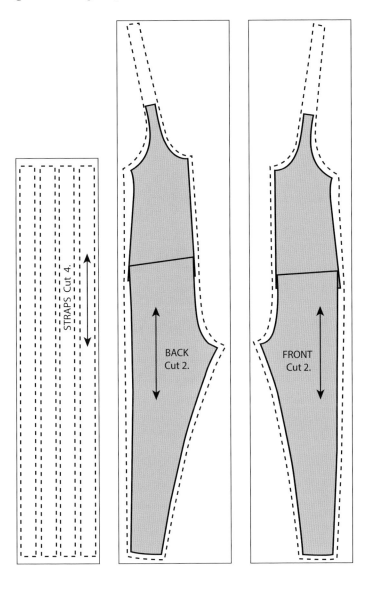

STRAPS Cut 4.

BACK
Cut 2.

FRONT
Cut 2.

Sewing

1 Sew the pieces together, extending the seams from the bottom to the top edges (see Sewing Trousers and Leggings, page 50).

2 Finish the armhole, strap, and neck edges (see Fabric Bands, page 24).

3 Hem the leg openings using your choice of hems (see Hemming, page 19). I used a zigzag-stitch finish.

WOVEN FABRIC JUMPSUIT

Marking and Cutting the Fabric

Fabric suggestions: Lightweight woven cotton, viscose, or silk

1. Use the trousers templates and tank top template.

2. Try on the trousers and tank top that you used to make the templates and see how much they overlap at the waist. Since this style is made in woven fabric, it is a good idea to make the overlap loose and a bit baggy so you can sit down in the jumpsuit comfortably.

3. Make the style markings as follows:

   Front and back jumpsuit: You'll need 2 copies of the tank top template to pair with the trousers front and back templates. Position the templates as shown, overlapping the tank top hem and trousers waist the desired overlap amount.

   To adapt the top of the jumpsuit, mark a line from the top side waist of the trousers up to the top center area of the tank top. From there, mark a straight line to meet the center seam. Use a seam allowance of ¾″ (1.9cm) for all the edges except for the center front and center back; use a more generous seam allowance to those edges, as shown.

   Straps: Mark 4 rectangles 4″ × 25″ (10cm × 63.5cm) for the straps. *Note:* I made the pieces narrower toward the top to make tying the ends together easier. You can vary the length and width of the straps.

4 From a double layer of fabric, mark and cut 2 jumpsuit fronts and 2 jumpsuit backs. From a single layer of fabric, mark and cut 4 straps.

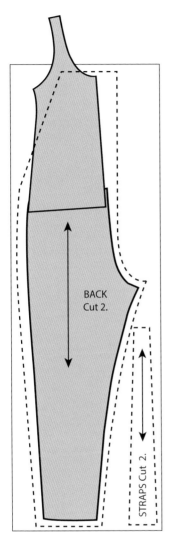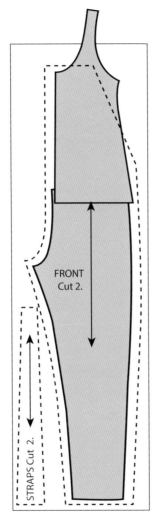

BACK
Cut 2.

FRONT
Cut 2.

STRAPS Cut 2.

STRAPS Cut 2.

Sewing

1 Sew the pieces together, extending the seams from the bottom to the top edges (see Sewing Trousers and Leggings, page 50).

2 Cleanly finish all the arm, back, and front neck openings by pressing the seam allowance to the wrong side and stitching it in place. Finish the edges of the straps the same way.

3 Stitch the bottom end of the straps to the front and back of the jumpsuit, as shown.

4 Hem the leg openings using your choice of hems (see Hemming, page 19).

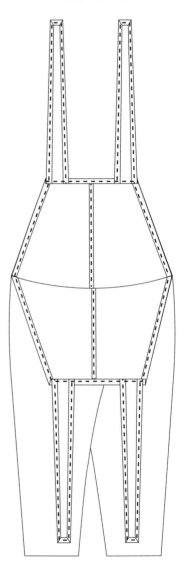

BASIC T-SHIRT DRESS

Marking and Cutting the Fabric

Suggested fabrics: Jersey or other stretch fabric

1 Use the T-shirt template. Fold the bottom corner of the sleeve template up so it easier to draw the underarm curve. Add a ½″–¾″ (1.3–1.9cm) seam allowance unless otherwise noted.

I suggest marking and cutting the neck opening so it is on the small side. This way you can make it wider and more open once you sew the front and back pieces together.

2 Make the style markings as follows:

Dress back: Place the template on the fabric fold and trace around it, extending the length and width at the hem, as shown. Draw the bottom line of the dress slightly curved as it meets the side seam.

Dress front: Trace the template to match the dress back, and mark the front neck opening, which is lower than the back neck opening.

3 Mark and cut 1 dress front and 1 dress back, both cut on the fabric fold.

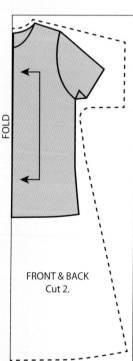

FOLD

FRONT & BACK
Cut 2.

VARIATION

For a looser fit, mark the sleeves longer and wider and add extra seam allowance along the side seam.

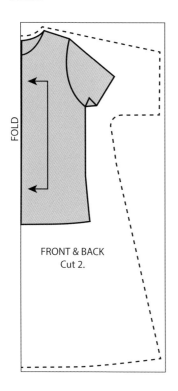

FOLD

FRONT & BACK
Cut 2.

Sewing

1 Sew the pieces together (see Sewing T-Shirts, Tops, and Dresses, page 47). Try on the garment and make any fit or design adjustments before finishing the edges.

2 Finish the edges as desired (see Edge Finishes, page 21). The neckline on the sample shown here was finished with the inside out edge finish (see Inside Out, page 22).

3 Hem the sleeves and bottom of the dress with a single-fold or double-fold hem (see Hemming, page 19). Topstitch with 1 or 2 rows of topstitching.

WOVEN DRESS WITH TIERS

Marking and Cutting the Fabric

Suggested fabrics: Lightweight woven fabric

1 Use the T-shirt template. Fold the bottom corner of the sleeve template up so it easier to draw the underarm curve. Since this dress is made with woven fabrics, you need to add at least 2″ (5.1cm) extra seam allowance on the sleeve and side seams. For a looser fit, add more width to the seam allowance. Use the standard ½″–¾″ (1.3–1.9cm) seam allowance on the neckline and shoulders.

2 Decide how long you want the dress and then decide how many tiers you wish to add. Make the dress as long or as short as you would like! Make the style markings as follows:

Dress back: Place the template on the fabric fold and trace around it, marking the desired length. Make the sleeve slightly wider.

Dress front: Trace the template to match the dress back, and mark the front neck opening, which is lower than the back neck opening.

Tiers: Follow the instructions for tier sizes in Making a Tiered Skirt (page 31).

3 Fold, mark, and cut the fabric to make 1 dress front and 1 dress back, both cut on the fabric fold. Mark and cut 2 (or 3) tiers on the fabric fold.

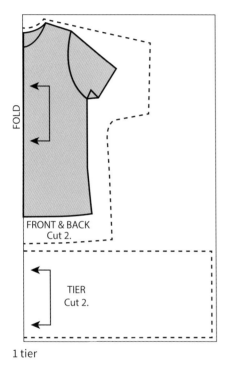

1 tier

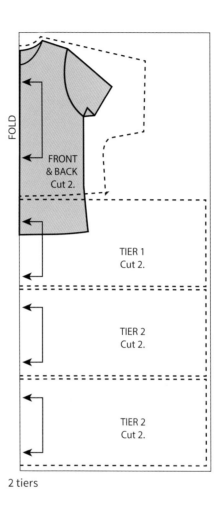

2 tiers

Sewing

1 Sew the dress front and dress back together (see Sewing T-Shirts, Tops, and Dresses, page 47).

2 Sew the tier pieces together to make 1 or 2 tiers. Gather and sew the first tier to the dress bottom. If using, gather and sew the second tier to the bottom of the first tier (see Gathering Fabric, page 29).

3 Finish the edges with your choice of finishes (see Edge Finishes, page 21). A zigzag stitch is an easy hem finish.

CIRCLE SKIRT DRESS

Marking and Cutting the Fabric

Fabric suggestions: Soft woven cotton or viscose

1 Use the T-shirt template for the dress front and
   back and the trousers back template for the
   skirt. Since this dress is made with woven fabrics,
   you need to add a least 2″ (5.1cm) extra seam
   allowance along the sleeve and side seams. For a
   looser fit, add more width to the seam allowance.
   Use the standard seam allowance of ½″–¾″
   (1.3–1.9cm) for the neckline and shoulders.

2 Follow the cutting
   instructions for the
   Woven Fabric Tops
   (page 60) to cut the
   dress top, *except*
   shorten the length of
   the cut pieces slightly.

3 Cut the skirt following
   the cutting instructions
   for the Circle Skirt
   (page 82).

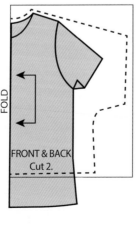

FOLD

FRONT & BACK
Cut 2.

Sewing

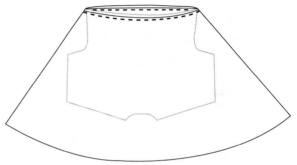

3 With right sides together, sew the skirt to the dress top. You will probably have to gather the top of the skirt slightly (see Gathering Fabric, page 29).

1 Sew the dress front and dress back together (see Sewing T-Shirts, Tops, and Dresses, page 47).

2 Finish the neckline using the bias tape edge-finishing technique (see Bias Tape, page 21).

4 Try on the garment and make any fit or design adjustments.

5 Hem the sleeves and skirt using your choice of techniques (see Hemming, page 19).

STRAP DRESS

Marking and Cutting the Fabric

Fabric suggestions: Jersey or other stretch fabric

1 Use the tank top template.

2 Make the style markings as follows:

Dress top:

• Mark the top of the dress slightly higher than half-way up the strap; you can always lower the design line for the neckline when you try on the dress.

• Draw a straight (not curved) line from the top edge to the armhole/side seam point and then continue the curve of the tank top down the side.

• Make the dress as long as you want.

You can always mark the side seam curve with a wider seam allowance so it won't be too tight over your hips. It's easy to take a dress in along the side seams.

3 Add the standard seam allowance of ½″–¾″ (1.3–1.9cm) to the edges except on the arm opening, where you need more space to make a straight line and not a curve.

4 Fold, mark, and cut the fabric to make 1 dress front and 1 dress back, both cut on the fabric fold.

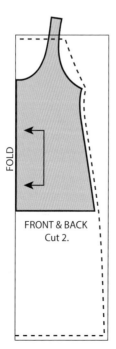

FOLD

FRONT & BACK
Cut 2.

Sewing

1   With right sides together, sew the side seams from the hemline up toward the arm opening, stopping ½″ (1.3cm) from the underarm point. Try on the dress and make any adjustments to the neckline or side seams.

2   Press the seam allowances at the neck and arm openings to the wrong side and stitch them in place.

3   This style shows 2 different types of straps. For both types, try on the dress and measure to determine how long to make the straps. The straps can be as wide as you would like.

Fabric or trim tape straps: To determine your strap length, measure from the top of the dress to the back of the dress and add 1″ (2.5cm) to that measurement. Cut 2 straps (or make 2 straps from fabric). Pin the ends of the straps ½″ (1.3cm) inside the top edge and back edge of the dress at the top corners, as shown. Make sure the straps aren't twisted. Stitch the straps to the dress. I stitched a small rectangle to make sure the straps were securely in place.

Decorative trim straps: With the dress on, make a circle with the trim, starting at the side seam and wrapping it up and around your shoulder back to the side seam. Make sure the trim is snug enough so that the dress doesn't sag and the trim doesn't slide off the shoulder. Add ½″ (1.3cm) to the trim length and stitch the narrow ends together to make a circle. Make 2 straps. Stitch to the arm opening of the dress using the knitted tape technique (see Knitted Tape, page 23), as shown.

4   Hem the dress using your choice of techniques (see Hemming, page 19).

A-LINE STRAP DRESS AND TOP

Marking and Cutting the Fabric

Fabric suggestions: Lightweight woven fabrics like cotton, viscose, satin, or silk

1 Use the tank top template.

2 Make the style markings as follows:

Dress front and back:

• Since the template was made from stretch fabric and this style is designed for woven fabrics, add extra seam allowance by placing the template 1″–2″ (2.5–5cm) away from the fabric fold.

• Fold the top of the template strap down 1″ (2.5cm).

• Draw a curved neckline from the fabric fold to just above the template strap.

• Draw a diagonal line from the top corner to the armhole / side seam point.

• Draw a line sweeping out toward the fabric edge to the desired length (for a dress or for a top) to create width and swing in the dress.

• Draw a gently curved bottom hemline.

3 Fold, mark, and cut the fabric to make 1 dress front and 1 dress back, both cut on the fold.

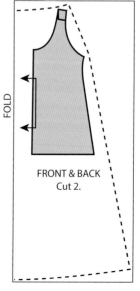

FOLD

FRONT & BACK
Cut 2.

Sewing

1 With right sides together, sew the side seams from the hemline up toward the arm opening, stopping ½″ (1.3cm) from the underarm point.

2 Press the seam allowances at the arm openings to the wrong side and stitch them in place.

3 Fold and press the front and back neck edges 1″–2″ (2.5–5cm) to the wrong side. Stitch on the finished edges to create casings for the ribbon or drawstring.

4 Use 35″ (89cm) of decorative ribbon, tape, or cording for the strap piece. Use a safety pin to feed the strap through the front casing and then through the back casing. Try on the dress to determine the strap length. Knot the ends then slide the knot into one of the casings so the knot is hidden.

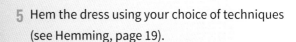

5 Hem the dress using your choice of techniques (see Hemming, page 19).

A-LINE TIE STRAP DRESS

Marking and Cutting the Fabric

Fabric suggestions: Jersey or other stretch fabric

1 Use the tank top template.

2 Make the style markings as follows:

Dress front and back:

• Draw the neckline curve of the dress higher than the tank top so it isn't too revealing. You can always make it lower once you have stitched it together and tried it on.

• Extend the straps approximately 10˝ (25.4cm) up from where the template ends so they are long enough to tie.

• Draw a line sweeping out from the underarm / side seam point toward the fabric edge to the desired length. This dress will have an A-line shape with lots of swing.

• Draw a gently curved bottom hemline.

3 Add the standard seam allowance of ½˝–¾˝ (1.3–1.9cm) to all the edges.

4 Fold, mark, and cut the fabric
to make 1 dress front and
1 dress back, both cut on the
fabric fold.

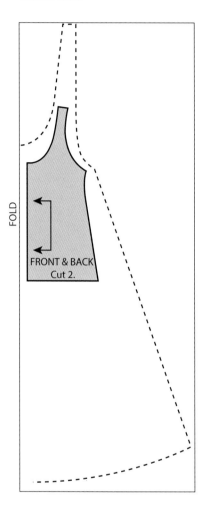

FOLD

FRONT & BACK
Cut 2.

Sewing

1 With right sides together, sew the side seams.

2 Try the dress on and tie the shoulder straps. Check to see if the
dress needs to be taken in on the side seams to be tighter or if
the neckline needs to be lowered for a more revealing look.

3 Finish the edges of the arm openings, neck edges, and the
straps with a zigzag stitch or use a serger.
Here a very narrow serger stitch is
used for a beautiful edge.

4 Hem the dress using your choice
of techniques (see Hemming,
page 19).

Tip

**Use contrasting thread to finish the
edges for design interest.**

A-LINE TIE STRAP RUFFLED DRESS

Marking and Cutting the Fabric

Fabric suggestions: Lightweight woven fabrics like cotton, viscose, and silk

1 Use the tank top template.

2 Decide on the length of the dress and the size of the ruffle.

3 Mark the cutting lines for the pieces following the instructions for the A-Line Tie Strap Dress, Marking and Cutting the Fabric (page 106). Adjust the length of the dress front and back so it is the desired length including the ruffle. Add the standard seam allowance of ½"–¾" (1.3–1.9cm).

4 Mark rectangles for the desired ruffle size (see Making a Tiered Skirt, page 31).

5 Cut the fabric to make 1 dress front and 1 dress back, both cut on the fabric fold. Cut also a rectangular piece (or pieces) for the ruffle.

FOLD

FRONT & BACK
Cut 2.

RUFFLES
Cut 2.

Sewing

1 With right sides together, sew the side seams.

2 Try the dress on and tie the shoulder straps. Check to see if the dress needs to be taken in along the side seams to be tighter or if the neckline needs to be lowered for a more revealing look.

3 Press the seam allowances at the neck, strap, and arm openings to the wrong side and stitch them in place.

4 Sew the ruffle pieces together. Gather and sew to the dress bottom (see Gathering Fabric, page 29).

5 Hem the ruffle using your choice of techniques (see Hemming, page 19).

A-Line Tie Strap Ruffled Dress

ASYMMETRICAL DRESS

Marking and Cutting the Fabric

Fabric suggestions: Jersey and other stretch fabrics

1 Use a tank top full template (see Making a Full Template, page 32).

2 Make the style markings as follows:

Dress front and back:

• Mark the desired length.

• Draw a diagonal line across one strap over to the top of the other strap.

• Draw a line down to the armhole / side seam point.

• Use the standard seam allowance of ½″–¾″ (1.3–1.9cm) on all the edges except along the armhole, where you need extra seam allowance.

• If desired, add extra seam allowance to the side seam curves so the dress has more width at the hips.

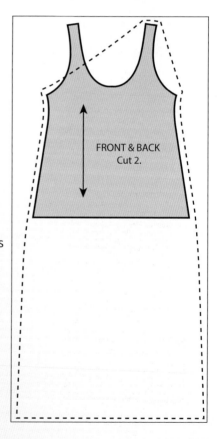

FRONT & BACK
Cut 2.

3 If you decide to add a hemline ruffle, shorten the dress accordingly. Mark rectangles for the desired size of ruffle (see Making a Tiered Skirt, page 31).

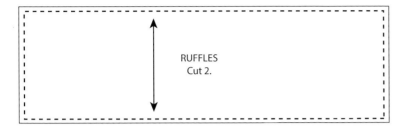

RUFFLES
Cut 2.

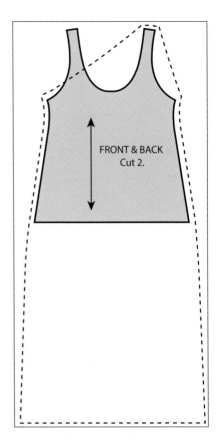

FRONT & BACK
Cut 2.

4 From a double layer of fabric, cut 1 dress back and 1 dress front. If using, cut the rectangles for the ruffle pieces.

Sewing

1 Sew the dress front and dress back with right sides together along the side seams and at the shoulder. Use a stretch stitch.

2 Try the dress on to see if you need to adjust the side seams or the shoulder seams to make the dress tighter or looser and to see if you want to lower or raise the asymmetrical neckline.

3 Finish the armhole edges and asymmetrical neckline with your choice of edge finish (see Edge Finishes, page 21). For this dress, I turned the edges ¼″ (6mm) to the wrong side and stitched the edge in place with a zigzag stitch.

4 If using, sew the ruffle pieces together. Gather and sew to the dress bottom (see Gathering Fabric, page 29).

5 Hem the dress or ruffle using your choice of techniques (see Hemming, page 19).

SWEATER DRESS AND TOP

Shown with Leggings (page 90)

Marking and Cutting the Fabric

Fabric suggestions: Jersey, isoli (French terry), interlock, or other stretch fabric

1 Use the sweater template.

2 Make the style markings as follows: Mark the chosen length; this style works from a cropped top to a dress of any length. Curve the bottom hemline slightly. Use the standard seam allowance of ½″–¾″ (1.3–1.9cm).

3 Decide how wide you want the neckband and cuffs. Mark the pieces:

   Width: 2 times the desired width plus 2 times the seam allowance

   Length: The measured length of the opening or slightly shorter

Tip

Make the neckband wider for a turtleneck look.

4 Fold, mark, and cut the fabric to make 1 front piece, 1 back piece, 2 sleeves, 1 neck piece, and 2 cuff pieces if using.

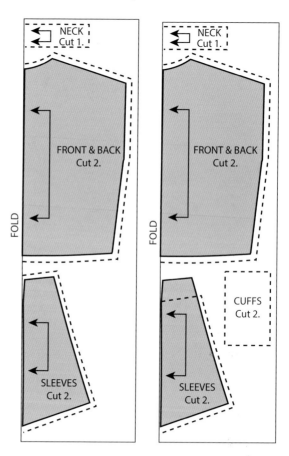

Variations

CREATE A DROPPED SHOULDER

For a more relaxed version, change the shape of the side seam and sleeve to make a dropped shoulder.

1 Add 2″ (5cm) extra seam allowance to the side and shoulder lines. Use the standard seam allowance of ½″–¾″ (1.3–1.9cm) for the neck and hem edges.

2 Mark the cutting lines for the sleeve as follows:

• B indicates the seamline for the drop sleeve.

• **Draw the sleeve** *width*: 2 times the B measurement plus 1″–2″ (2.5–5cm) for a very loose fit.

• **Draw the sleeve** *length*: The length of the sleeve template for a normal folded hem *or* 2″ (5cm) shorter to add a band or cuffs.

• **Mark the cuff:** The same measurement as the sleeve edge by 2 times the desired length plus standard seam allowance

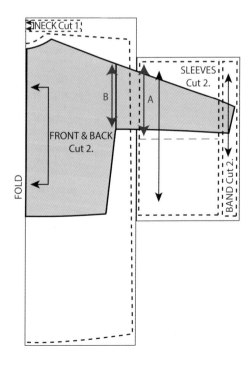

LOOSER AND LONGER VARIATIONS

For a loose fit: Add more seam allowance to the sides and under the arm for a boxy and loose fit. An extra seam allowance of 2″ (5cm) is a good start. Change the markings for a dropped shoulder if desired (see Create a Dropped Shoulder, page 114).

For a longer version: Make the markings longer and straight down. Change the markings for a dropped shoulder if desired (see Create a Dropped Shoulder, page 114).

Sewing

1 Sew the front, back, and sleeve pieces together (see Sewing Sweaters and Garments with Sleeves, page 48).

2 Sew the neckband and cuffs, if using (see Fabric Bands, page 24).

3 Hem the bottom edges with your choice of technique (see Hemming, page 19).

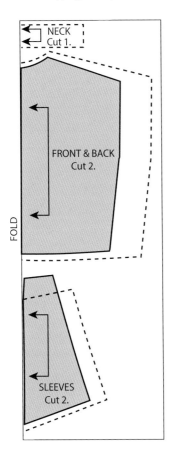

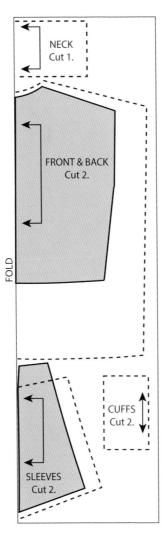

Sweater Dress and Top

KIMONO

Shown with Faux Wrap Box Skirt (page 85)
and Faux Wrap Ruffle Skirt (page 83)

Marking and Cutting the Fabric

Fabric suggestions: All types of fabric, woven or knit

1 Use the sweater template.

2 Decide how long you want the kimono and how long you want the sleeves, or make them however long the fabric length/width allows. Add the standard seam allowance of ½″–¾″ (1.3–1.9cm) to all edges except for the marked shoulder, underarm, and side seams; add 2″ (5cm) seam allowance to those edges.

3 Make the style markings as follows:

Back: Draw the style lines boxier than the template, extending the shoulder line so it is straight instead of diagonal. Make the sleeve opening straight and more open. Add more seam allowance to the underarm and side seam.

Front: Follow the shape, length, and sleeve length of the kimono back. Be sure to trace the template's front neck marking. Position the center front at least 1″ (2.5cm) from the fabric fold. Use a ruler to mark a straight line from the neck/shoulder point down to the hemline.

Neck / front opening bands: You can make the bands as wide as you would like. Add 2 times the seam allowance to the chosen width. Mark the length 2 times the new center front opening plus 2 times the back neck opening plus 2 × the seam allowance. Mark the desired width and length as shown, replacing the template center front and neckline.

Optional sleeve bands: Mark 2 bands, each the measurement of the sleeve opening plus the seam allowance by the desired width plus seam allowance.

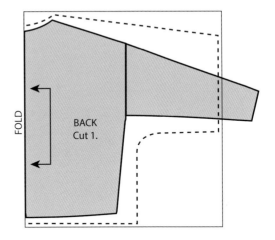

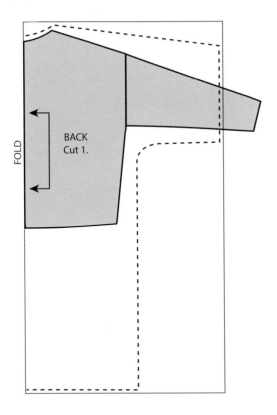

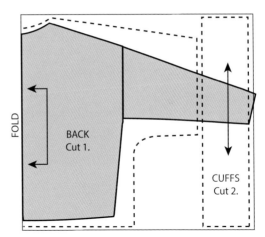

4 Fold, mark, and cut the fabric to make 1 back, cut on the fabric fold; 2 fronts; and 2 bands for the neck and front opening.

Sewing

1 Sew the back and 2 front pieces with right sides together on the shoulder seam. Sew the sleeve bands to the sleeves, if using. Sew the side seams of the back and front pieces together, starting from the sleeve openings to the bottom edges.

2 Piece the band pieces as necessary to make 1 long piece. Fold it in half lengthwise with wrong sides together, and zigzag or serge the long raw edges together. Also fold and stitch the sleeve bands, if using.

3 Fold the band in half, matching the ends to find the center. Position the center of the band at the center back neck edge of the kimono, so the raw edge of the kimono opening aligns with the zigzag or serged seam of the band. Pin or clip the band to the front / neck opening with right sides facing each other.

4 Sew the band to the front / neck opening. Extend the folded edge of the band out and toward the kimono opening. Topstitch close to the seam to help the band stay flat and in place.

5 Hem the sleeve openings (if not using the bands) and the bottom edge with your choice of technique (see Hemming, page 19).

COATIGANS AND CARDIGANS

Marking and Cutting the Fabric

Fabric suggestions: Jersey, isoli (French terry), sweater knits, interlock, and other stretch fabrics

1 Use the sweater template. Add a ½″–¾″ (1.3–1.9cm) seam allowance to the neckline and sleeves.

2 Make the style markings as follows:

Front: Draw a line straight down from the shoulder point to the desired length. Draw a straight hemline from the side seam to the center front. This piece is placed on the fabric fold but will then be cut apart along the fabric fold to make 2 front pieces. Be sure to trace the front neckline markings.

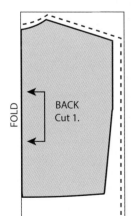

Back: Draw the same line from the shoulder point to the desired length and the hemline, as for the front. Be sure to trace the back neckline. Cut this piece on the fabric fold to make 1 back.

Sleeves: Place the sleeve template on the fabric fold and trace.

3 Fold, mark, and cut the fabric to make 2 front pieces, 1 back piece, and 2 sleeves cut on the fabric fold.

Loose-Fitting Variations

For a loose fit, add extra seam allowance at the side seams and sleeves; 2″ (5cm) is a standard amount to add. You can shorten the sleeves and/or create a dropped shoulder (see Create a Dropped Shoulder, page 114).

For an even roomier fit, follow the instructions for making a dropped shoulder (see Create a Dropped Shoulder, page 114). Also cut the front of the cardigan wider by adding 2″ (5cm) to the center front, and curve the bottom hemline slightly, as shown.

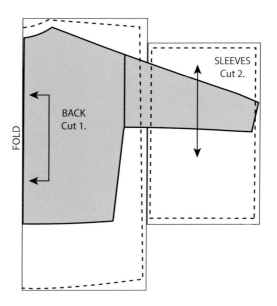

Sewing

1 Sew the pieces together (see Sewing Sweaters and Garments with Sleeves, page 48).

2 Use your choice of finishes for the neckline and front openings (see Edge Finishes, page 21). I used knitted trim (see Knitted Tape, page 23).

3 You can also use bias tape to
   finish the neck and center front
   openings (see Bias Tape, page 21).

4 Hem the sleeves and bottom
   edges with your choice of
   technique (see Hemming,
   page 19).

PONCHO

Marking and Cutting the Fabric

Fabric suggestions: Fleece, wool, faux fur, or thick isoli, or other warm and comfy fabrics (Reversible fabric looks great, too!)

1 Use the sweater template.

2 Fold the fabric in half lengthwise and then fold again to make 4 layers, with folds on the side and at the top.

3 Mark 1 poncho piece on both folds that is as long and as wide as the fabric allows (you can always shorten it once you try it on). Trace the neckline with a ½″–¾″ (1.3–1.9cm) seam allowance. Draw a curve at the lower corner. Cut 1 poncho piece.

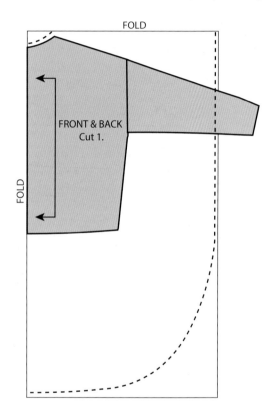

4 Try the poncho on and mark directly on the fabric if and where you want to make the neck opening larger. The opening can be more of a boatneck shape so it is easy to pull the poncho over your head. Also check whether you want to shorten the sleeve edge or hemline (by cutting evenly around the outside edges).

Sewing

1 Finish the neck opening with your choice of finishes (see Edge Finishes, page 21). I used a knitted tape (see Knitted Tape, page 23).

2 Hem the bottom edges with your choice of techniques (see Hemming, page 19).

PONCHO WITH COLLAR

Marking and Cutting the Fabric

Fabric suggestions: Fleece, wool, faux fur, thick isoli, or other warm and comfy fabrics

1 Use the sweater template.

2 Follow Poncho, Marking and Cutting the Fabric, Steps 2 and 3 (pages 123 and 124) to mark and cut 1 poncho piece.

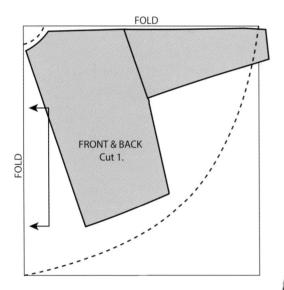

FOLD

FOLD

FRONT & BACK
Cut 1.

3 Try on the poncho and mark directly on the fabric if and where you want to make the neck opening larger so it is easy to pull the poncho over your head. You might want to cut the neckline so it is more open since you will be attaching a collar. Also check whether you want to shorten the sleeve edge or hemline (by cutting evenly around the outside edges).

4 The collar needs to overlap itself, so cut 1 rectangular piece the size of the circumference of the neck opening plus ⅓ of the circumference extra. The width of the rectangle should be 2 times the desired height of the collar plus 2 times the seam allowance.

Sewing

1 Fold the collar in half lengthwise with right sides together. Sew the ends and turn the collar right side out.

2 Mark the center of the collar on the open side, and pin or clip that marking to the center back of the poncho inside the neck opening. Continue pinning or clipping the open edges of the collar to the neckline; the finished edges of the collar will overlap in the front. Stitch the collar to the poncho.

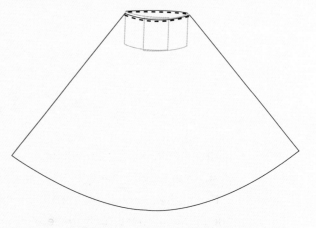

3 Hem the bottom of the poncho (see Hemming, page 19).

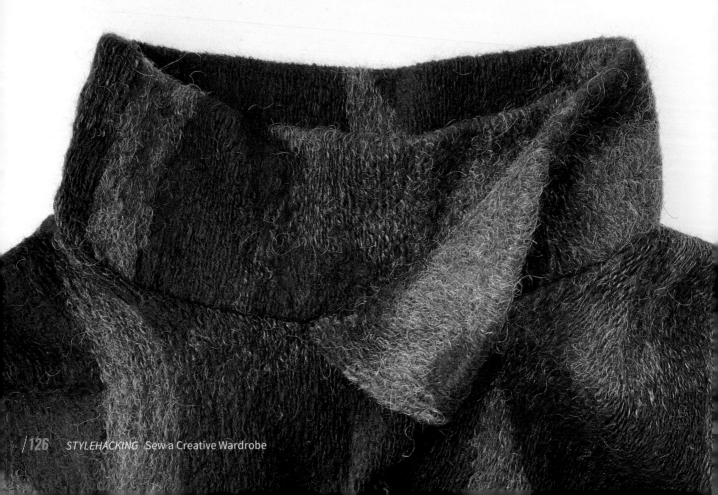

About the Author

KAROLINE DAHRLING HUGHES is a designer and creator living in a small town in the northern part of Denmark. She blogs and uses every opportunity to be creative and to inspire others to do the same. She has published a sewing book in Danish, but this is her first book in English.

Visit Karoline online!

Blog: skandimama.com

Facebook: /skandimama.karoline

Instagram: @karoline.skandimama